An Introduction to Evidence-Based Design

EXPLORING HEALTHCARE AND DESIGN

edac™

Second Edition

This is the second edition of Study Guide One: An Introduction to Evidence-Based Design: Exploring Healthcare and Design. Although some of the content has been updated, this will not impact the EDAC examination.

Request for permission should be addressed to:
The Center for Health Design
1850 Gateway Boulevard, Suite 1083, Concord, CA 94520
925-521-9404, 925-521-9405 (fax), admin@healthdesign.org

Includes appendices, glossary, references, and an index
First published 2008

Published by
The Center for Health Design
1850 Gateway Boulevard, Suite 1083
Concord, CA 94520
925-521-9404

Printed by
The Graphics Resource
3262 La Canada
Lafayette, CA 94549
510-813-1447

Printed in the U.S.A.
ISBN: 978-0-9819005-1-3

EDAC
Study Guide Series

**STUDY GUIDE ① **
An Introduction to Evidence-Based Design
Exploring Healthcare and Design

**STUDY GUIDE ② **
Building the Evidence Base
Understanding Research in Healthcare Design

**STUDY GUIDE ③ **
Integrating Evidence-Based Design
Practicing the Healthcare Design Process

HOW TO USE THIS STUDY GUIDE

This guide provides you with an introduction
to evidence-based design in healthcare.
Each chapter ends with a series of questions.
The questions are provided for you to determine
your understanding of the material that will
appear on the EDAC exam. Answers for the
questions are provided in the back of the book.

For more information on EDAC, visit
The Center for Health Design Web site at
www.healthdesign.org/edac

Contents

Foreword

What you are about to read is, in part, the cumulative result of over three years of work by more than 100 volunteers. We are an interdisciplinary group of healthcare and design professionals who, like you, passionately believe that an evidence-based design process has the power to help transform how healthcare is delivered today. We believe that patients should be able to devote their energies to getting well without having to fight their environments. We believe that nurses and doctors should be able to go to work every day and not worry about getting sick or injured because of the design of the environment. We believe that sustainable buildings don't have to cost more. We believe that evidence-based design is not just a marketing tool but something that can actually help save people's lives.

From the beginning, our mission has been to develop a community of accredited industry individuals through educational assessment of an evidence-based design process. We call this Evidence-Based Design Accreditation and Certification, or EDAC. Several years, countless hours, and many challenges later, our vision is even loftier. We hope there comes a time when all healthcare environments are created using an evidence-based design process.

We think that the timing for EDAC couldn't be more perfect. Our industry has come a long way in terms of what we understand about the impact of the built environment on the quality of healthcare: a great deal of information, a growing body of research, and many theories about evidence-based design. For us, this progress has been remarkable, but it is still not enough. The EBD context or process has not been defined or standardized yet. And until now, no benchmarks have existed for measuring a professional's capabilities and knowledge of the most current thinking in this area. As the body of knowledge grows, we think it is critical that the collective body of evidence be applied competently and credibly to build better buildings.

This study guide series serves as an excellent compendium of the current state of our industry as well as a valuable roadmap to where we need to set our sites for the future. Book One provides a history of EBD in addition to an overview of the forces shaping healthcare today. This background information is necessary for a clear understanding of Books Two and Three, which look at the research and design process. All three guides are designed to serve as scholastic works on their own, outside of the EDAC movement. You can use these guides as much to prepare for the EDAC accreditation exam as to round out your knowledge of an evidence-based design process for healthcare facilities.

You may be asking yourself what EDAC means for you. If you have been engaged in this process for several years, you might have already noticed a difference in the industry. As a community, there is still much work to be done to achieve the level of rigor we are all striving for. Looking forward, EDAC means new and higher expectations from all of us about what we design every day. It also means we must influence the decision makers and shoulder our way into the consciousness of the public. EDAC means we must change healthcare for the better.

We hope you will share our passion, embrace the process, and become changemakers in the industry and champions of the evidence-based design process. Your engagement is critical to its success, no matter what part of our industry you serve.

How will we know when our vision for EDAC is a reality? When all hospitals and other healthcare facilities are designed and built using the most current research and thinking to support the people that spend time in them. Will we ever accomplish this? Probably never, because what we know about EBD as a process is constantly evolving. But, with EDAC, our hope is that the evolution will be noticeable, positive, and significant. By reading these study guides and engaging in EDAC, you're part of making that change happen. We passionately believe that EDAC will prepare any interested healthcare and design professional to understand and apply the components of EBD. We urge you to learn all you can.

Our thanks go out to The Robert Wood Johnson Foundation for providing initial funding to this project and to The Center for Health Design and its board of directors and staff for their unwavering support. In particular, we want to thank Debra Levin for her leadership in making this dream a reality.

–EDAC Volunteers, November, 2008

Acknowledgments

The development and production of this book was made possible through a partnership with Nurture by Steelcase. Special thanks to Phyllis Goetz and her team at Nurture for their contributions in the development of EDAC and their ongoing support of The Center for Health Design and its programs.

Special recognition goes to the Military Health System for generously contributing information from the publication: Evidence-Based Design: Application in the MHS. This document provided the foundation for a significant amount of the guides' content.

We are indebted to the following people who participated as co-authors of this guide and who devoted many days and nights to develop the content:

Eileen B. Malone, RN, MSN, MS, EDAC, senior partner at Mercury Healthcare Consulting LLC

Constance Harmsen, RN, MS, MHA, FACHE, EDAC, chief executive officer, Surgical Specialty Hospital of Arizona, and consultant, health and safety design, Joint Commission Resources

Karen (Kathy) Reno, PhD, MBA, RN , EDAC, consultant for Joint Commission Resources and Joint Commission International and assistant clinical professor for the College of Nursing, University of Illinois at Chicago

Eve Edelstein, PhD, FAAA, Assoc. AIA, EDAC, visiting scholar at the University of California, San Diego; adjunct professor at the NewSchool of Architecture and Design; and research associate with the Academy of Neuroscience for Architecture

D. Kirk Hamilton, FAIA, FACHA, EDAC, associate professor of architecture at Texas A&M University

Alberto Salvatore, AIA, NCARB, EDAC, principal and cofounder of Salvatore Associates

Julie R. Mann-Dooks, senior staff, Noblis Center for Health Innovation, Public Sector

Charisse Oland, MHA, RD, FACHE, EDAC, chief executive officer, Rehabilitation Hospital of Wisconsin

Phyllis Goetz, PDAC, EDAC, global director, A & D, Nurture by Steelcase

Pierre Michiels, EDAC, regional healthcare manager, Nurture by Steelcase

Eleanor Lee, MAIBC, EDAC, director, Capital Projects, Provincial Health Services Authority

Addie Johnson, EDAC, PhD candidate, University of Wisconsin, Milwaukee

Anjali Joseph, PhD, EDAC, director of research, The Center for Health Design

Thanks to Upali Nanda, PhD, EDAC, vice president and director of research at American Art Resources for developing the original outline for this book. The dedication of people like her make CHD's work possible.

List of Figures

List of Tables

BY THE END OF THIS CHAPTER, YOU SHOULD BE ABLE TO:

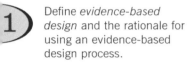

1 Define *evidence-based design* and the rationale for using an evidence-based design process.

2 List the key steps of the evidence-based design process.

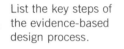

3 Identify and describe trends influencing healthcare today and explain how they can be addressed by the use of evidence-based design.

4 Understand the history and evolution of evidence-based design.

Chapter One at a Glance

Embracing Evidence-Based Design

Making the Business Case

State of Healthcare Today: Key Trends and Challenges

Evidence-Based Design: Its Roots and Evolution

State of the EBD Process Today

Chapter One Review Questions

Chapter One Quiz Questions

1

An Introduction to Evidence-Based Design

▪▪ EMBRACING EVIDENCE-BASED DESIGN

Without a doubt, healthcare represents the most personal and complex service provided: intimate personal information must be shared with strangers; complex and often frightening and painful tests and procedures must be performed; life-and-death decisions are constantly made; the staff speaks an entirely different language; and the buildings are daunting and difficult to navigate.

Because most healthcare occurs in a facility, stakeholders have a duty to understand that the building itself can help to reduce the stress experienced by patients, their families, and the healthcare teams caring for them. The healthcare environment is a work environment for the staff, a healing environment for patients and families, a business environment for the provision of healthcare, and a cultural environment for the organization to fulfill its mission and vision (Stichler, 2007). In order to realize these environments, facility designs must be linked to the organization's goals and objectives.

Additionally, stakeholders need to understand how design can help produce the preferred healthcare outcomes being sought and mitigate the untoward results now plaguing the industry. Errors are not just statistics. Every mistake has a face, a story, and consequences for the patient, his or her family, and the care delivery team. Evidence-based design (EBD) provides another important intervention in a bundle of solutions to improve desired outcomes.

The desire to create healing environments can be traced back to the vestiges of European medicine. The asclepieion hospital, built in ancient Epidaurus, a small city in Ancient Greece, in the sixth century BCE, included patient rooms that faced eastward to promote healing and was the most celebrated healing center of the Classical world. While the decision to orient the rooms toward the sun was done intuitively, on what basis are current healthcare-facility design decisions made?

Historically (and aside from intuition), most healthcare design has been driven by previous design experiences of the engaged architectural firm, the personal clinical and administrative experiences of the client, and changes in technology, rather than solid research findings. Aside from a greater market share (for example, from a new building with the latest diagnostic or technology-related services), little association has been made between these enormous investments and meaningful healthcare industry measures.

Until recently, building infrastructure was regarded as a sunk or overhead cost, rather than a revenue-producing variable. This view resulted from the inability to link facility resources with the heart of the healthcare business: providing safe, quality patient care and family support, and a positive and safe work environment for staff.

Roger Ulrich (1984) began to change this line of thinking with his pioneering study of the effects of hospital window views on recovery from abdominal cholecystectomy surgery. Ulrich's study focused on patients who could see trees, rather than a brick wall, through their patient-room window. The study found that these patients subsequently required less narcotic pain medication, experienced a shorter hospital stay, and had fewer negative evaluative comments in nurses' notes.

More than 20 years have passed since that initial study, and as the healthcare industry has evolved, so too has EBD. According to Stichler and Hamilton (2008, p. 3):

> The term *evidence-based design* evolved from other disciplines that have used an evidence-based model to guide decisions and practices in their respective fields … One of the first formal and widely accepted definitions of evidence-based medicine, for example, was put forth by Sackett, Rosenberg, Gray, Hanes, and Richardson (1996), who stated that "Evidence-based medicine [EBM] is the conscientious, explicit, and judicious use of current best evidence in making decisions about the care of individual patients. The practice of [evidence-based] medicine means integrating individual clinical expertise with the best available evidence from systematic research" (p. 71).

In 2003, healthcare architect Kirk Hamilton first attempted to formalize a definition of the term, *evidence-based design*. He described the role of the designer and the process by stating, "An evidence-based designer makes decisions—with an informed client—based on the best available information from credible research and evaluations of projects. Critical thinking is required to draw rational inferences about design from information that seldom fits a unique situation precisely" (Hamilton, 2004, para. 2).

In his article, Four Levels of Evidence-Based Practice in the AIA Journal of Architecture (2004), Hamilton writes:

> The process works especially well in the healthcare field. It appeals to physicians, who practice based on medical evidence. It gives patients and families higher-quality experiences. It

appeals to business-minded administrators by reducing costs and improving organizational effectiveness. It helps hospital boards as they seek evidence to justify costly decisions. And it benefits the public, consumer groups, and those paying the bills as they seek effective, lower-cost health care (para. 3).

Hamilton also defined four levels of EBD practices by healthcare designers. Practitioners at the first level of EBD keep up with the literature and apply the evidence to inform their designs, looking for success stories when the project is complete. Hamilton contends that serious practitioners of EBD must go farther. In addition to literature review and interpretation of research findings for the purpose of design, practitioners at level two predict the outcomes expected from their design—thus developing design hypotheses—and commit to measurements that will confirm or disprove their predictions. Practitioners at level three commit to hypothesis and measurement while adding a commitment to share their findings publicly. At level four, practitioners increase rigor by publishing their results in peer-reviewed venues (Hamilton, 2008).

Hamilton's most current definition, which borrows from Sackett et al (1996), is: "Evidence-based design is a process for the conscientious, explicit, and judicious use of current best evidence from research and practice in making critical decisions, together with an informed client, about the design of each individual and unique project" (Stichler & Hamilton, 2008, p. 3).

It is clear that the definition of EBD has evolved since its inception, reflecting knowledge gained through the application of the EBD process. Based on these earlier definitions of EBD, The Center for Health Design (2008) defines EBD as "the process of basing decisions about the built environment on credible research to achieve the best possible outcomes."

Keep in mind that the word *design* should be considered in its broadest sense, which is, "a plan or scheme conceived in the mind and intended for subsequent execution" (Oxford English Dictionary, 2000), rather than just the production of a facility blueprint.

Several developments in the healthcare industry in the last 10 years have made it critical to understand how the physical environment is a part of the bundle of strategies to improve the quality of care. The first decade of the 21st century began with the seminal report from the Institute of Medicine (IOM) in 2000, *To Err Is Human: Building a Safer Health System*, which broke the silence around medical errors and posited that adverse events are the eighth leading cause of death in America, killing an estimated 98,000 individuals each year. Since the physical environment can potentially contribute to or aggravate these problems, it is essential for healthcare design teams to closely examine the relationship between building design and patient, staff, family, and environmental outcomes.

IOM's 2000 report was quickly followed by a second volume, *Crossing the Quality Chasm: A New Health System for the 21st Century*. This second volume has provided the agenda for healthcare system transformation that depends on new facility designs (IOM, 2001). The IOM healthcare quality aims are shown in Figure 1.

■■ MAKING THE BUSINESS CASE

With the $240 billion investment in healthcare construction expected between 2009 and 2013, this call for a transformation is perfectly timed (Jones, 2009). "Health care construction will likely see a small decline in 2009 and 2010. However, it will remain at a historically high level" (p. 8). According to Reed Construction Data (2010):

Spending for healthcare is projected to drop 6% this year, increase 12-13% next year and then rise at about the typical 8%

annual pace for non-recession years. The value of hospital construction starts is forecast to fall 3% this year, rise 5% next year and then expand through 2014 at a 5-6% pace. The value of construction starts for residential care facilities will drop 8% this year, 1% next year, rebound 50% in 2012-13 and then begin to decline slowly for several years (Haughey, 2010, Reed Construction Data web site).

The goal is to determine how healthcare facility investments contribute to improvements in patient-care quality and the safety and satisfaction of both patients and staff while positively enhancing the bottom line. Further, as the healthcare industry is on the brink of this construction boom, it is also facing a number of significant changes and challenges, many of which encourage the use of EBD.

Figure 1:
Institute of Medicine (IOM) Quality Aims

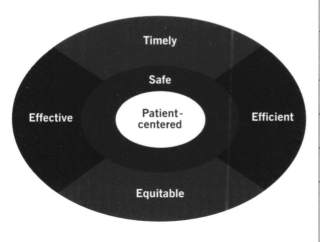

	Patient-centered–provision of care that is respectful and responsive to patient preferences and needs, ensuring that patient values guide clinical decisions.
	Effective–provision of services based on scientific knowledge to all who can benefit; not providing services to those not likely to benefit.
	Efficient–avoidance of waste, including waste of equipment, supplies, ideas, and energy.
	Safe–avoidance of injuries to patients from the care that is intended to help them.
	Timely–reduction of waits and harmful delays for both those who receive and those who give care.
	Equitable–provision of care that does not vary in quality with respect to gender, ethnicity, geographic location, and socio economic status or other personal characteristics.

Reprinted with permission from Joint Commission Resource (Henriksen, Isaacson, Sadler, & Zimring, 2007).

The Business Case for Better Hospitals

With mounting pressure to improve quality and safety and growing evidence that the design of the physical environment can contribute to both, why haven't all hospitals rushed out and implemented EBD innovations? Some have. For those that have not, the barriers are often perceived to be economic. The need to balance one-time construction costs against ongoing operating savings and revenue enhancements is central to making the business case for EBD innovations.

The first attempt to analyze this balance was published in 2004 by a multidisciplinary team that reviewed published research and the actual experience of healthcare organizations that utilized EBD in portions of their construction projects (Berry et al, 2004). Many of these pioneering organizations were part of a collaborative research program initiative called The Pebble Project™, founded by The Center for Health Design.

After reviewing the research, the team designed a hypothetical hospital (which they called the Fable Hospital®). When they analyzed the Fable's operating cost savings resulting from design innovations that could be shown to reduce infections, eliminate unnecessary patient transfers, minimize patient falls, lower drug costs, lessen employee turnover rates, as well as improve market share and philanthropy, they concluded that, with effective management and monitoring, the financial operating benefits would continue for several years (Berry et al, 2004). This result would make the additional innovations a sound long-term investment. In short, there was a compelling business case for building better, safer hospitals.

—*Blair L. Sadler, Jennifer DuBose, and Craig Zimring, "The Business Case for Building Better Hospitals through Evidence-Based Design,"* Health Environments Research and Design Journal, *Vol. 1, No. 3.*

■■ STATE OF HEALTHCARE TODAY: KEY TRENDS AND CHALLENGES

Seven major trends impact healthcare today:

Trend One: Public Focus on Quality and Patient Safety
Trend Two: Healthcare Costs and Reimbursement
Trend Three: Aging Population and Caregiver Shortages
Trend Four: Health Information Technology
Trend Five: Genomics and Technology
Trend Six: Disaster Preparedness and Emergency
      Room Saturation
Trend Seven: Environmental Safety and Sustainability

Clearly, these are not all the trends that impact the healthcare industry. Although additional trends will emerge, these seven trends currently represent major challenges for healthcare. EBD has the ability to positively influence these challenges; therefore an individual using an EBD process should maintain awareness of current trends and consider their impact on healthcare design. EBD can influence the challenges these seven trends present by:

- Reducing medical errors and, therefore, costs of care that emanate from latent conditions within the physical design
- Improving satisfaction and efficiency of caregivers, especially aging caregivers, thereby helping recruitment and retention of a scarce and essential resource
- Designing a supportive physical environment for health information technology, reengineered work processes, and new diagnostic and interventional technologies
- Providing innovative, adaptable designs to maximize response to natural and human-made disasters.

Trend One: Public Focus on Quality and Patient Safety

The World Health Organization (WHO) states that "no

adverse event should ever occur anywhere in the world if the knowledge exists to prevent it from happening" (World Health Organization Collaborating Centre for Patient Safety Solutions Web site, 2010). Following up on the IOM report on patient safety, HealthGrades (2008) reported on patient safety errors in Medicare patients between 2004 and 2006. The study analyzed 41 million Medicare hospitalization records from nearly all US hospitals and found almost 1.1 million patient safety errors that resulted in 238,337 potentially preventable deaths and cost approximately $8.8 billion.

Further, preventable adverse drug events (ADEs) occur 380,000 to 450,000 times per year in hospitals, 800,000 times per year in long-term care facilities, and 530,000 times per year in outpatient settings for Medicare patients (IOM, 2006). None of these studies included errors of omission (that is, the failure to prescribe medications in cases where they were necessary). The IOM concluded that at least 1.5 million preventable ADEs occur in the United States each year. In addition, healthcare-associated infections (HAIs) are increasing in the United States and are perceived by many as the greatest risk patients face in a hospital.

Healthcare-associated infections are infections that patients acquire during the course of receiving treatment for other conditions within a healthcare setting. According to the CDC, the frequency of HAIs varies by body site. Of the infections reported among patients, the most common HAIs are urinary tract infections (32%), surgical-site infections (22%), pneumonias (15%), and bloodstream infections (14%) (CDC, 2008).

Due in part to statistics such as these, national organizations are taking notice. The Joint Commission (The Joint Commission Web Site, 2010) has made reduction of healthcare associated infections one of its 2010 National Patient Safety Goals (NPSGs).

The Centers for Disease Control and Prevention (CDC) now refer to HAIs more generically—as a health care-associated infection (Horan, Andrus, & Dudeck, 2008).

The Centers for Disease Control and Prevention (CDC) estimates that nearly 2 million people, or 1 in 20 hospitalized patients, experience a healthcare-associated infection (HAI) every year in the United States, leading to approximately 88,000 deaths (Ranji et al, 2007). According to Scott (2009), "the overall annual direct medical costs of HAI to US hospitals ranges from $28.4 to $33.8 billion (after adjusting to 2007 dollars using the Consumer Price Index for all urban consumers) and $35.7 billion to $45 billion (after adjusting to 2007 dollars using the Consumer Price Index for inpatient hospital services)" (para 2).

The Institute for Healthcare Improvement (IHI, 2008) articulated practices to prevent HAIs, specifically surgical-site infections, central-line-associated bloodstream infections, and ventilator-associated pneumonia, as three of the six interventions in its 100,000 Lives Campaign. The IHI announced a national initiative in December 2004 to engage thousands of hospitals in the United States in an effort to prevent 100,000 unnecessary inpatient deaths through improvements in care via six clinical interventions. In June 2006, the IHI estimated that 122,300 unnecessary deaths were avoided in the participating hospitals. Subsequently, IHI launched its 5 Million Lives Campaign, an initiative to protect patients from 5 million incidents of medical harm from 2006 to 2008. Upon the formal closure of the campaign in December 2008, 4,050 hospitals were enrolled. Over 2,000 facilities used the campaign's twelve interventions to "reduce infection, surgical complication, medication errors, and other forms of unreliable care in facilities" (The Institute for Healthcare Improvement web site, 2010).

The IOM (2003) report, *Priority Areas for National Action: Transforming Health Care Quality*, recognized the prevention of HAIs as 1 of the 20 priority areas for national action. As of 2009, the Centers for Medicare and Medicaid Services (CMS) will withhold reimbursement for the following HAIs: catheter-associated urinary tract infections, Staphylococcus aureus bloodstream infections, and surgical-site infections (Wachter, Foster, & Dudley, 2008).

In 2004, the IOM published *Keeping Patients Safe: Transforming the Work Environment of Nurses*. Its main point is thus: How well people are cared for by their nurses affects their health; therefore, efforts to take good care of nurses will also significantly impact the healthcare system for the better and improve patient safety. One of its major recommendations focused on the design of the workspace for caregivers to prevent and mitigate errors. The report noted that the physical features of inpatient facilities can interfere with efficient nursing work and decrease patient safety. Poor layout of patient-care units, patient rooms with poor design, and inadequate deployment of communication technologies decrease the time nurses have available to assess and provide direct care to their patients (Page, 2004).

Along with the increased spotlight on patient safety is a trend toward mandated reporting of patient experiences in hospitals. According to Sadler, DuBose, and Zimring (2008), the CMS and the Agency for Health Research and Quality (AHRQ) provided support to develop The Hospital Care Quality Information from the Consumer Perspective (HCAHPS) survey. This survey was developed to:

- "produce comparable data on patients' perspectives of care on topics that are important to consumers;
- create incentives for hospitals to improve care through public reporting; and
- increase public accountability through increased transparency of quality of care" (Sadler, et al, 2008, p. 24).

Sadler et al (2008), "Although there are no data available yet to report from this new trend, it seems reasonable to predict that hospitals with more comfortable, safe, and patient-centered physical environments will be rated higher by patients in the HCAHPS survey, and this could have significant influence on a patient's choice of hospitals, with a resulting impact on hospital's market share and financial situation" (p. 24).

More information about quality and patient safety is being made available to the public. In 2008, the US Department of Health and Human Services (HHS), CMS, and the Hospital Quality Alliance refined their website Hospital Compare (*www.hospitalcompare.hhs.gov*), allowing consumers to compare US hospitals based on quality and patient satisfaction measures.

Many efforts have occurred nationally and within hospitals attempting to decrease the number of unnecessary deaths in the United States. Actions have focused on discovering why such errors occur, how to prevent them, creating organizational cultures of safety, patient-safety data collection, support for new information technology for healthcare delivery, and public dissemination of safety information to consumers and providers.

Trend Two: Healthcare Costs and Reimbursement

The Commonwealth Fund Commission on a High Performance Health System IOM report (Schoen, How, Weinbaum, Craig, & Davis, 2006) concluded that with its wealth of high-tech equipment, the US system delivers some of the best medical care in the world.

However, this care comes at a cost. The United States spends more on healthcare than any other nation in the world—$2.26 trillion in 2007, which is 15.2% of the gross domestic product (GDP) (Health Systems Resources, 2008). Since 1970, healthcare spending has grown at an average annual rate of almost 10% and is projected to be 19.5% of the GDP in 2017 (Health Systems Resources, 2008).

Yet, despite this spending, the US healthcare system is filled with inefficiencies, leaves tens of millions uninsured, and creates an environment filled with disparities and inequalities. Reasons for this include a pervasive lack of accountability, inadequate funding for information technology, and a payment system that rewards inefficiency. Across 37 indicators of performance, the United States achieved an overall score of 66 out of a possible 100 when comparing actual national performance to achievable benchmarks (Commonwealth Fund, 2006).

According to The Commonwealth Fund (2010), "health care reform legislation—the Patient Protection and Affordable Care Act and the Health Care and Education Affordability Reconciliation Act—includes numerous provisions to expand access to health insurance, improve the quality and comprehensiveness of coverage, and make coverage more affordable for all Americans (para. 1)." Between 2010 and 2018, numerous insurance provisions will be enacted as part of this healthcare legislation. It is too soon to tell what impact this legislation will have on healthcare delivery and costs.

The HealthLeaders Media Industry Survey 2010, a cross-sector survey, reports that respondents (CEOs, CFOs, and quality officers) continue to rank quality and safety as a top priority; however, the priority of cost reduction is on the rise. "For 2010, cost reduction has moved up to Priority No. 3, selected by 35% of CEOs [up from No. 6]" (HealthLeaders Media, 2010, pg. 4). While capital healthcare building projects are seen as a sunk cost, the incorporation of evidence-based design strategies can often result in a positive return on investment.

Increased healthcare costs in the United States are associated with the aging population and new medical technology—the procedures, equipment, drugs, and processes through which healthcare is delivered (Kaiser Family Foundation, 2007). Life expectancy increased by 7 years between 1960 and 2000, but in the past 20 years, the medical costs for each year of life gain increased markedly, especially in older age groups. At 65 years of age, the cost per year of life gained was $121,000 between 1980 and 1990 and $145,000 between 1990 and 2000 (Cutler, Rosen, & Vijan, 2006). On average, the increases in medical spending since 1960 are deemed to have provided reasonable value; yet spending increases in medical care since 1980 are also a cause for concern (Cutler, Rosen, & Vijan, 2006).

Healthcare Reimbursement: Financing the Cost of Care

Healthcare costs include doctor visits, hospital stays, surgery, procedures, tests, home care, and other treatments and services. The purpose of health insurance is to help people cover these healthcare costs.

Health insurance pays for all or part of an individual's healthcare bills, if the person is insured. Types of health insurance include group health plans, individual plans, workers' compensation, and government health plans such as Medicare and Medicaid. Health insurance can be further classified into fee for service and managed care. Both group and individual insurance plans can be either fee-for-service or managed-care plans. Types of managed-care plans include health maintenance organizations (HMOs) and preferred provider organizations (PPOs). The insurance company, government agency, or managed-care organization is often called the third-party payer; a transaction occurs between a patient and a healthcare provider, and the payer is the third party between them (Austin & Wetle, 2008).

Payment methods for healthcare fall under two broad categories: fee for service or capitation. There are several primary fee-for-service reimbursement methods: cost-based reimbursement, charge-based reimbursement (few payers reimburse full charges to a provider), and negotiated or discounted charges. While most fee-for-service reimbursement strategies reward the amount of services used, capitation rewards less utilization of services as a set fee is paid to the provider per covered life (Gapenski, 2007).

In spite of the value of advances in medical care, the strain upon personal, corporate, and government pocketbooks requires people to ask how much healthcare the nation can afford. New models of reimbursement are being discussed. Cost-effectiveness analysis via nonbiased, well-controlled research studies comparing the benefits and costs of technology need to occur (Neumann et al, 2008).

In addition to these economic issues, hospitals and other healthcare institutions are facing significant changes to the reimbursement landscape.

- For instance, in September 2006, the American Hospital Association (AHA) established a policy that calls for hospitals to share information with the public about healthcare pricing and guidelines for reporting and defining charity care and community benefit reporting. On the issue of pricing transparency, the AHA asked hospitals to work with state hospital associations to expand existing efforts that make information about hospital charges available to consumers.

  Hospitals and state associations are encouraged to work with insurers to provide information about a patient's out-of-pocket costs before a medical visit, participate with federally led research to determine what type of pricing information consumers want, and create consumer-friendly pricing language for common terms, definitions, and explanations (Colmers, 2007; DoBias, 2006).

- In August 2006, President Bush signed an executive order requiring four federal agencies—the departments of Health and Human Services, Defense, Veterans Affairs and Federal Employees Health Benefit Program—to compile and share quality and cost information on the healthcare services they pay for and make that information public.

  As of January 1, 2007, these agencies were required to share patient medical information, develop with the private sector and other government agencies measures to gauge the quality of care and to enact them, make available to beneficiaries the dollar amount agencies spend on common procedures, and identify practices that promote high-quality healthcare (Arizona Hospital and Healthcare Association, 2006).

• Sadler et al (2008) state: Over the past few years, value-based purchasing, or pay for performance, has emerged. Pay for performance will "have a profound impact on the business case for quality improvement, including the physical environment in which people work and care is received" (p. 23).

Pay for performance (P4P) is a method to foster quality performance. The current pay system for healthcare in America creates many incentives for a high volume of services yet few for better health. P4P is viewed as an important mechanism that can help transform the payment system into one that rewards higher value and better outcomes (Weems, 2008). Careful attention must be given to the design of a P4P system because it could influence far more than just payment rates.

• The National Quality Forum has identified "Never Events" that are largely preventable and should simply never occur in hospitals (National Quality Forum, 2006). CMS has identified specific harms, including infections and falls that should not be reimbursed (Arnon et al, 2006). While the details are just emerging, it is likely that within 3 to 5 years, virtually no payers will reimburse hospitals and physicians for serious harm that they caused. In addition, consumers will have easier access to clear, comparable outcome measures and will be able to make choices about where they go for care based on this information. Increasingly, consumers will be channeled to payer-preferred networks based on quality measures.

Poorly performing hospitals could risk losing significant market share (Sadler, B., DuBose, J., Malone, E., & Zimring, C., 2008, p.4).

Sadler et al (2008) state that:

Medicaid programs and commercial payers will likely follow the CMS lead and begin to announce that they will not reimburse hospitals for harm that they cause … Consumers will have easy access to clear outcome measures and will make choices about where to go for their care based on this information (p. 24).

Further, Sadler, DuBose, and Malone (2008) explain that:

In this new era of transparency and public reporting, hospitals in some states have voluntarily decided not to charge payers and patients for errors committed by hospitals … The connection between such a policy and an organization's reputation is important. In addition, the connection between hospital errors and the incidence of litigation has been effectively described (Gosfield and Reinertsen, 2005). The hospital associations of Minnesota and Massachusetts have adopted a no-charge-for-errors policy in advance of the CMS rules taking effect, and many other states will likely follow (Beaudoin, 2007, p. 4).

They (Sadler et al, 2008) conclude, "We are entering a new era—one in which patients and payers will no longer pay for poor performance" (p. 24).

Trend Three: Aging Population and Caregiver Shortages

More than a million people turn 60 years old each month worldwide. It is projected that the US population will grow 18% between 2000 and 2020, with a 65% growth in the population over 65 years of age. This is the age group that requires a disproportionately larger share of healthcare services. By 2050, three times as many people in the world will be age 60 years and over—an increase from 600 million to 2 billion (Cohen, 2006; Hatcher, 2006). Sadler (2009) argues, "The coming of age of the Baby Boomer generation as major consumers of healthcare cannot be ignored. They represent a significant attitudinal shift from the passive patients of prior generations to outspoken consumers. In addition to expecting top-quality healthcare professionals and state-of-the-art technology, they will expect the care that they and their families receive to be provided in supportive, calming environments that feel more like home" (p. 102).

Nurses are an aging population also. Today, the average age of the nurse is 46.7. By 2010, 40% of the US nursing work force will be over 50 years old. Further, it is projected that in 2020, there will be a shortage of more than 800,000 nurses. These combined realties will result in more elderly people needing healthcare and an inadequate number of older nurses to take care of them (Cohen, 2006; Hatcher, 2006).

The healthcare workforce is exposed to various occupational hazards on a daily basis. They are exposed to airborne infections in the hospital as well as those acquired through direct contact with patients. Taking care of patients in the hospital is often back-breaking work with nurses required to manually lift heavy patient loads. This is an issue of great concern today with the increasing bariatric population in US hospitals. In addition, other environmental stressors such as high noise levels, inadequate light, poor air quality and poorly designed workspaces impact staff health and safety. Proper design of healthcare settings along with a culture that prioritizes the health and safety of the care team through its policies and values can reduce the risk of disease and injury to hospital staff and provide the necessary support to perform critical tasks.

Nurses are not the only caregivers expected to be in short supply. By 2020 a shortage of 96,000 physicians is predicted for the United States. Reasons for the shortage include declining satisfaction with the profession, decreasing reimbursement, rising medical malpractice rates, and the higher premium younger physician graduates place on having balance and a high quality of life.

Trend Four: Health Information Technology
Studies published by the IOM and others demonstrate that fragmented, disorganized, and inaccessible clinical information adversely affects the quality of healthcare and compromises patient safety (GAO, 2006).

The use of health information technology (HIT)—the management of medical information and its secure exchange among consumers and providers—has enormous potential to improve the quality of healthcare and is critical to improving the performance of the US healthcare system. (GAO, 2006).

Health information technology (HIT) provides the umbrella framework to describe the comprehensive management of health information and its secure exchange between consumers, providers, government and quality entities, and insurers. Health information technology (HIT) in general are increasingly viewed as the most promising tool for improving the overall quality, safety and efficiency of the health delivery system (Chaudhry et al, 2006). Broad and consistent utilization of HIT will:

• improve health care quality
• prevent medical errors
• reduce health care costs
• increase administrative efficiencies
• decrease paperwork
• expand access to affordable care

Interoperable health IT will improve individual patient care, but it will also bring many public health benefits including:

- Early detection of infectious disease outbreaks around the country
- Improved tracking of chronic disease management
- Evaluation of health care based on value enabled by the collection of de-identified price and quality information that can be compared" (Wikipedia, 2010 para 1-4)

The federal government has taken a leadership role in driving change to improve the quality and effectiveness of healthcare, including the adoption of HIT. The American Recovery and Reinvestment Act of 2009: "provides approximately $19 billion for Medicare and Medicaid Health IT incentives over five years. [Among other things, the Act]:

- Officially establishes the Office of the National Coordinator for Health Information Technology (ONCHIT) within HHS to promote the development of a nationwide interoperable Health IT infrastructure; President Bush already created ONCHIT by Executive Order in 2004.
- Establishes Health IT Policy and Standards Committees that are comprised of public and private stakeholders (for example, physicians) to provide recommendations on the Health IT policy framework, standards, implementation specifications, and certification criteria for electronic exchange and use of health information.
- Provides financial incentives through the Medicare program to encourage physicians and hospitals to adopt and use certified electronic health records (EHR) in a meaningful way (as defined by the Secretary and may include reporting quality measures). Authorizes ONCHIT to provide competitive grants to states for loans to providers" (American Medical Association Web site, 2010).

Technologies such as the electronic medical record and bar coding of human, drug, and biological product labels have demonstrated financial savings and reduction of medical errors. For example, Banner Health implemented a comprehensive, IT-enabled care transformation project that included a full electronic medical record and computerized physician order entry at its new non-replacement hospital, Banner Estrella Medical Center, which opened in January 2005. A rigorous, conservative approach was used to identify and measure the benefits of the system with a $2.6 million annual bottom-line impact reported (Hensing et al, 2008). The savings emanated from key performance indicators including the following:

- avoidance of adverse drug events
- reduction in medication-related claims
- pharmacy cost reduction
- elimination of forms
- document storage costs reduction
- reduction in days in AR
- increase in nurse retention
- overtime reduction
- reduction in ED patients leaving without treatment

Health Insurance Portability and Accountability Act (HIPAA)

The Health Insurance Portability and Accountability Act of 1996 mandates improved efficiency in healthcare delivery by standardizing electronic data interchange as well as the protection of confidentiality and the security of health data through setting and enforcing standards.

More specifically, HIPAA called upon the Department of Health and Human Services to publish new rules to ensure the following:

- Standardization of electronic patient health, administrative, and financial data
- Unique health identifiers for individuals, employers, health plans, and healthcare providers
- Security standards protecting the confidentiality and integrity of individually identifiable health information—past, present, or future

All healthcare organizations—including healthcare providers, health plans, public health authorities, healthcare clearinghouses, and self-insured employers, as well as life insurers, information system vendors, various service organizations, and universities—are required to comply with HIPAA regulations.

Practically speaking, the passage of HIPAA meant sweeping changes for most healthcare transactions and administrative information systems as well as implications for design, such as changes to the built environment to support patient privacy and data security systems. While HIPAA is primarily concerned with the confidentiality of health data and electronic sources of information, the role of the environment in protecting privacy and confidentiality is also critical. In addition, healthcare organizations are concerned with ensuring that others cannot access health data pertaining to individual patients.

Another important contribution of HIT to healthcare is the growing use of evidence-based medicine, practice, and management. With the power of the computer to store and retrieve easily the most current research regarding clinical practice, physicians, nurses, and consumers are informing themselves of this evidence to make better healthcare decisions and treatment choices.

HIT has also contributed other benefits such as shorter hospital stays, faster communication of test results, improved management of chronic diseases, and improved accuracy in capturing charges associated with diagnostic and procedure codes (Aspinall & Hamermesh, 2007). However, due to significant financial, technical, cultural, and legal barriers such as lack of access to capital, a lack of data standards, and resistance from healthcare providers, only a small number of US healthcare providers have fully adopted HIT (GAO, 2006).

Trend Five: Genomics and Technology

Genomics (the study of genes and their implementation in the development of healthcare products) and personalized medicine, new diagnostic equipment, and telemedicine advances will impact the healthcare delivery system. Technical advances in molecular medicine, the use of technology, and diverse engineering disciplines have the power to transform the practice of medicine beyond recognition in the coming two decades.

At the same time, however, financial, sociocultural, and political forces will be actively attempting to impose new policies for professionals and institutions on clinical practice. Personalized medicine will enable the right diagnosis to be made at the outset of the disease, diseases will be caught and treated earlier, and molecular profiling will better assure the right treatment for the patient, matched to his or her unique genetic profile, thereby decreasing adverse reactions (Aspinall & Hamermesh, 2007). Prospective medicine will provide a much-needed focus on prevention and proactive action, as people will have vital information about predisposition to serious diseases later in life. While the impact of genomics is affecting healthcare now, its greatest impact is clearly yet to come.

New diagnostic equipment is getting smaller via nanotechnology and is able to visualize more clearly all types of body structures. Smaller equipment decreases the need for invasive procedures, with their greater risk of complications. Telemedicine has the capacity to connect the world in new ways. Rural healthcare clinics, homes, schools, churches, community hospitals, and academic centers can be linked on a global basis with telemedicine. Robotics guided via tele-connection links can allow an expert physician in one part of the world to guide another practitioner or even perform a complex procedure in another part of the world.

Trend Six: Disaster Preparedness and Emergency Room Saturation

Emergency-care systems in the United States include pre-hospital emergency services, hospital emergency departments (ED), freestanding urgent-care centers, and emergency response teams dispatched for disasters, such as Hurricane Katrina and the terrorist attacks on September 11.

Emergency medical and mental health conditions are treated within this system. The demand for emergency care has grown 26% between 1993 and 2003 in the United States, while the number of EDs declined by 425 and the number of hospital beds declined by 198,000 over the same time period. EDs and trauma centers are overcrowded, and the majority of ED patients (78%) are walk-in patients (Rodriguez & Aguiree, 2006).

Use of the emergency healthcare system has increased due to several factors, including the increasing numbers of uninsured in the United States, the aging population, and increased use of drugs, in particular, methamphetamines. Saturation of the ED has occurred due to the shortage of nurses, physicians, and hospital beds. ED waiting room times often average 6 to 8 hours (Rodriguez & Aguiree, 2006).

The emergency healthcare delivery system is already at or over capacity and is ill-prepared to handle a major disaster (Rodriguez & Aguiree, 2006). "Floods, earthquakes, and other natural disasters, such as the [2010] earthquake in Haiti, take a terrible toll on human life, as can infectious disease outbreaks and man-made disasters like chemical spills or radiation accidents" (Zensius, 2010, p. 40). The threat of human-made disasters, such as terrorism, or natural disasters, such as hurricanes and outbreaks of viruses, are quite real. For example, the CDC has reported 400 cases of the avian flu in humans since 2003. If this were to spread, it would become a pandemic (CDC, 2008). When such disasters occur, the already overloaded emergency healthcare system staggers to respond. A recent study by the Center for Studying Health System Change found that hospitals in 12 nationally representative communities questioned their capacity to handle a large-scale disaster or epidemic (Rodriguez & Aguiree, 2006).

Trend Seven: Environmental Safety and Sustainability

The healthcare sector impacts community and global health through excessive energy consumption and the widespread use of hazardous and toxic chemicals. At an ecological level, healthcare facilities consume a huge amount of energy and materials in their construction and operation and generate a large quantity of toxic waste. There are serious concerns that patients and staff might sustain long term harm as a result of the toxic materials used in the very environments that are meant to be healing and therapeutic. Healthcare is the second highest energy-intensive industry after food service (Energy Information Administration, 2010, www.eia.doe.gov/emeu/consumptionbriefs/cbecs/pbawebsite/contents.htm#TotalEnergyFigureF, para. 5).

Hospitals use 836 trillion BTUs of energy annually and have more than 2.5 times the energy intensity and carbon dioxide emissions of commercial office buildings, producing more than 30 pounds of CO_2 emissions per square foot. Reducing the energy intensity of this sector will decrease its carbon footprint and also alleviate stress on America's electric power infrastructure

... New energy efficiency strategies hold the promise of re-duced costs for the sector, as US hospitals spend over $5 billion annually on energy, often equaling 1 to 3 percent of a typical hospital's operating budget or an estimated 15 percent of prof-its" (Department of Energy News Release, April 29, 2009).

If the United States is going to reduce its environmental impact to a sustainable level, it must substantially improve the environ-mental performance of healthcare. In addition to being large con-sumers and producers of energy, healthcare organizations are also waste creators. The volume of waste created includes such things as construction debris, medications, and surplus medical equip-ment. Practice Greenhealth describes the volume of water usage and waste creation and discusses the benefits of reducing both:

Hospitals and health care facilities are significant users of water. ... Health care facility water use varies widely de-pending on type, size, geographical location, and water use equipment/practices. A water use study published in 2002 showed a range of water use from 68,750 to 298,013 gallons per year per bed for hospitals in the size range of 133 to 510 beds (Practice Greenhealth). The nation's hospitals gener-ate approximately 6,600 tons of waste per day ... As much as 80 to 85% of a health care facility's waste is non-hazardous solid waste. Reducing water use can lead to major savings in terms of lower water and sewer bills ... In addition, many wa-ter conservation techniques can be directly linked to reduced energy consumption, resulting in even greater cost savings. (Practice Greenhealth, 2010).

According to Roberts and Guenther (2006),

Sustainable development is the most vibrant and powerful force to impact the building design and construction field in more than a decade (Cassidy, 2003). In every market sector, building owners, architects, and constructors are transforming the US construction industry.

Fueled by the success of the US Green Building Council's Leadership in Energy and Environmental Design (LEED) rating system, growing federal and state tax credit programs, and public and private financial energy incentives, more than 4.5% of construction activity in the United States is seeking to define sustainable building (Lounsbury, 2003). The healthcare sector faces unique opportunities and challenges as the construction industry increases its understanding of the impact of the built environment and operations on the health of building occupants, local communities, and global ecosystems (Roberts and Guenther, 2006, p. 81).

Further, say Roberts and Guenther (2006):

The healthcare industry has an essential role to play in developing buildings that demonstrate the economic, social, and environmental benefits of green building in the context of high-performance healing environments … As the healthcare industry's environmental footprint negatively affects the environment, these environmental impacts may in turn affect human health, and human health issues further increase the need for healthcare services. This is the center of the sustainability challenge. Improved environmental performance may contribute to an improved community health status (p. 82).

Can healthcare organizations afford to build green? A better question may be, can they afford not to? The *2006 AIA Guidelines for Design and Construction of Health Care Facilities* include references to sustainable and EBD practice, and an increasing number of state and local governments are requiring building design to meet LEED requirements ... For healthcare, the compelling links between buildings and health, the irony of a healthcare system that may contribute to environmental illness, and a strong connection to healthcare's fundamental mission to '"first do no harm" make sustainable building an important goal that is impossible to ignore (p. 104).

As stated earlier, the EBD process can help organizations face these challenging trends by designing healing and therapeutic environments that help reduce errors, improve patient and staff satisfaction, enhance efficiency, and support the latest technological advances such as HIT and genomics.

■I EVIDENCE-BASED DESIGN: ITS ROOTS AND EVOLUTION

Many forces have converged in the last 30 years to create the field of EBD. The EBD timeline (Figure 2) depicts the key events that have shaped EBD (Malone, Mann-Dooks & Strauss, 2007). EBD is structured in part along the lines of the evidence-based movement, which began in the 1970s with Professor Archie Cochrane's book "Effectiveness and Efficiency: Random Reflections on Health Services (1972), which highlights his work to collect, codify, and disseminate the "evidence" gathered in randomized control trials. A Canadian research group, led by professors Sackett and Guyatt at McMaster University in Ontario, Canada, subsequently established research methodologies to determine the best medical evidence in patient care that would ultimately be translated into practice, resulting in patient-care improvements (Cochrane, 1972).

However much of the evidence in EBD has been built up over the last 50 years by researchers working in the field of environmental psychology and related multidisciplinary fields such as environment and behavior that includes architects, interior

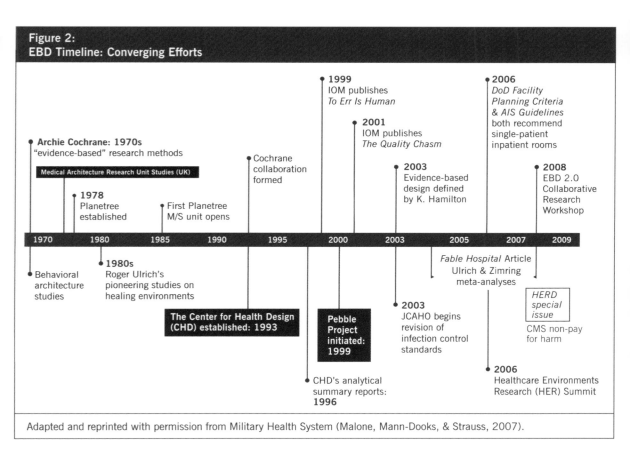

Figure 2:
EBD Timeline: Converging Efforts

Archie Cochrane: 1970s
"evidence-based" research methods

Medical Architecture Research Unit Studies (UK)

1978
Planetree
established

First Planetree
M/S unit opens

Cochrane
collaboration
formed

1999
IOM publishes
To Err Is Human

2001
IOM publishes
The Quality Chasm

2003
Evidence-based
design defined
by K. Hamilton

2006
*DoD Facility
Planning Criteria
& AIS Guidelines*
both recommend
single-patient
inpatient rooms

2008
EBD 2.0
Collaborative
Research
Workshop

1970   1980   1985   1990   1995   2000   2003   2005   2007   2009

Behavioral
architecture
studies

1980s
Roger Ulrich's
pioneering studies on
healing environments

The Center for Health Design
(CHD) established: 1993

Pebble
Project
initiated:
1999

2003
JCAHO begins
revision of
infection control
standards

Fable Hospital Article
Ulrich & Zimring
meta-analyses

*HERD
special
issue*

CMS non-pay
for harm

CHD's analytical
summary reports:
1996

2006
Healthcare Environments
Research (HER) Summit

Adapted and reprinted with permission from Military Health System (Malone, Mann-Dooks, & Strauss, 2007).

designers, sociologists, anthropologists, and others. As Zimring
et al (2008) stated recently:

EBD is a refinement of several strong, continuing research
and building delivery practices that have been active since the
1960s. For example, architectural researchers in the United
States and Britain have studied the impact of hospital layout
on workforce effectiveness since the 1970s (Clipson & Johnson, 1987; Clipson & Wehrer, 1973; Medical Architecture
Research Unit, 1971, 1973a, 1973b, 1976, 1977).

Environmental social scientists have studied issues such as wayfinding and patient and visitor experience (Carpman & Grant, 1993). Architectural researchers have explored how post-occupancy evaluation—the evaluation of occupied buildings—can inform design and building delivery (Baird, Gray, Issaacs, Kernohan, & McIndoe, 1996; Zimring, 2002) (Zimring, 2008, p. 12).

There are numerous relevant studies in environmental psychology and environment and behavior that can be found in journals such as *Environment and Behavior* and *Journal of Architectural & Planning Research* and in the annual meetings and proceedings of the Environmental Design Research Association (EDRA).

Another event that has been critical for the development of EBD was the start of the patient-centered care movement which began in the late 1970s in the United States with the establishment of the nonprofit organization Planetree.

As stated previously, Roger Ulrich published his pioneering study on the effects of a natural view on patient healing in 1984. In the same year, the first Planetree hospital was constructed.

Over the last 15 years, these various forces have converged to become the discipline now known as EBD. In 1993, a new organization named The Center for Health Design (CHD) formed with the express intention to serve as a consortium for knowledge in the many different fields (neuroscience, behavioral architecture, biology, psychology, neuro-immunology) that contribute to the creation of healing environments for both patients and staff.

In 1996, CHD published the first meta-analysis on the topic of EBD in a report sponsored by Armstrong World Industries, Jain Malkin, and WHR Architects. The report (Rubin, Owens, &

The Planetree model of care is a patient-centered, holistic approach to healthcare, promoting mental, emotional, spiritual, social, and physical healing. It empowers patients and families through the exchange of information and encourages a healing partnership with caregivers. It seeks to maximize positive healthcare outcomes by integrating optimal medical therapies into the healing environment. — Planetree Website (www.planetree.org/about.html)

In 2009, Planetree embarked on a journey to partner with design organizations that were unique in their approach to creating patient-centered, staff-supportive, and family-friendly environments called the Visionary Design Network. -EDAC Newsflash (www.healthdesign.org/edac).

Golden, 1996) found that there were 84 relevant research studies about the built environment. A 2004 update funded by the Robert Wood Johnson Foundation (RWJF) analyzed and catalogued more than 600 additional studies (Ulrich, Zimring, Joseph, Quan, & Choudhury, 2004). Another analysis of the literature from 2004 to 2007 has just been completed (Ulrich, Zimring, Zhu et al, 2008), which stated "The review found a growing body of rigorous studies to guide healthcare design ... The state of knowledge of evidence-based healthcare design has grown rapidly in recent years. The evidence indicates that well-designed physical settings play an important role in making hospitals safer and more healing for patients, and better places for staff to work" (Ulrich, et al, 2008, p. 61).

In 1997, a volunteer task force of CHD's Environmental Standards Council (ESC) used the information and data collected from the first EBD report as a basis for developing design recommendations and examples for the Joint Commission's "Management of Care" chapter of the accreditation manual for hospitals. The recommendations were incorporated into the 1999 edition of the manual.

At the same time that the Institute of Medicine (IOM) published its *To Err Is Human* report on quality and safety in 1999, CHD launched the Pebble Project, a joint research effort between CHD and healthcare providers. The purpose of the work is to cause a ripple effect in the healthcare industry by demonstrating how healthcare organizations have improved their specific outcomes by using an EBD process. The Pebble Project hospitals (more than 50 to date) are applying EBD to their renovations or new constructions, measuring their outcomes, and publishing their results in peer-reviewed journals (CHD, 2008a).

The Joint Commission (2005) responded to the IOM reports by creating a resource for healthcare organizations titled, *Infection Control Issues in the Environment of Care*. The goal of this 2005 publication was to inform healthcare organization personnel about healthcare-associated infections and how they can be minimized or prevented.

In that same year, the ESC drafted and submitted additions to the "Environment of Care" chapter for the 2006 *AIA Guidelines for Design and Construction of Health Care Facilities*. The chapter outlines the environmental factors that contribute to patient, staff, and family satisfaction, as well as increased safety, lower medical errors, and a better financial bottom line (2006 AIA Guidelines for Design and Construction of Health Care Facilities, 2006). The Health Guidelines Revision Committee unanimously accepted the recommendation for single-patient rooms for inpatients, as well as other evidence-based features for inclusion in these guidelines, which are updated every four years. The ESC will continue to add to future guidelines issues.

In 2007, the AIA's annual Healthcare Architecture Conference also converged with the annual Healthcare Design Conference produced by Vendome Group in association with CHD, a multidisciplinary learning event that offered educational content in healthcare design.

Also in 2007, Vendome Group and CHD launched the *Health Environments Research and Design Journal* (HERD), an interdisciplinary, peer-reviewed journal whose mission is to enhance the knowledge and practice of evidence-based healthcare design by disseminating research findings, discussing issues and trends, and translating research into practice. In 2008, *A Review of the Research Literature on Evidence-Based Healthcare Design* was published in HERD. Approximately 1,500 studies related to evidence-based design are now available (Ulrich & Zimring, 2008).

In 2006, professionals from academia, healthcare organizations, and CHD met in Georgia at the Health Environments Research Summit and, subsequently, in March 2008 at EBD 2.0 Collaborative

Research Workshop, to focus on the development of a coherent set of research initiatives that would have the potential to improve a range of clinical, safety, and organizational outcomes through the refinement of hundreds of EBD research ideas. Eight main EBD topics were identified. Participants prioritized the top two research initiatives for each topic area, the results of which are in Table 1.

Table 1: EBD Research Initiatives Identified at the EBD 2.0 Collaborative Research Workshop Proceedings in March 2008	
Group	**Top Two Research Initiatives**
Team 1: Nursing Station Design Typology	• What is the most appropriate nursing station configuration (centralized, decentralized, distributed) for medical/surgical and intensive-care units? • Only one research initiative identified
Team 2: Work-Force Efficiency and Effectiveness	• What is the relationship of departmental adjacencies and access to medical supplies, equipment, expertise, and unit configuration on work-force efficiency and effectiveness? • What is the impact of same-handed or standardized clinical, treatment, diagnostic, interventional, and surgical rooms upon staff efficiency and effectiveness?
Team 3: Patient Room	• Impact of acuity-adaptable rooms • Impact of information technology on patient room
Team 4: Work-Force Retention	• Does unit layout configuration and design encourage team interaction and mutual respect (physicians, nurses, other caregivers, and family members) and improve caregiver satisfaction, retention, and learning? • Does access to natural light, healing gardens, acoustics, etc., have an effect on caregiver satisfaction and retention?
Team 5: Hospital-Acquired Infections	• Patient-care-area materials' impact on HAI rates • What is the role of air quality in reducing HAIs?
Team 6: Patient Falls and Injuries	• Bathroom-related design and patient falls • Observation and patient falls
Team 7: Medical Errors	• The impact of noise on medical errors • Impact of information technology on medical errors
Team 8: Work-Force Health and Safety	• Staff control of the work environment • Lift design and workplace ergonomics
Reprinted with permission from The Georgia Institute of Technology.	

■■ STATE OF THE EBD PROCESS TODAY

Over the years, a number of approaches to the EBD process have emerged as pioneering organizations have taken the nascent knowledge and adapted it to their unique set of circumstances. However, the common thread in all the approaches is that EBD needs to be integrated into different stages of a typical building design process. Listed below are the key steps that have emerged as the EBD process.

- Define evidence-based goals and objectives.
- Find sources for relevant evidence.
- Critically interpret relevant evidence.
- Create and innovate evidence-based design concepts.
- Develop a hypothesis.
- Collect baseline performance measures.
- Monitor implementation of design and construction.
- Measure post-occupancy performance results.

The incorporation of these steps into practice requires the collaboration of healthcare organizations, design firms, and research expertise. Zimring, Augenbroe, Malone, and Sadler (2008) state:

> At the core of EBD is a fundamental shift in the way healthcare organizations think about, deliver, and manage buildings. Rather than simply being regarded as cost centers, in EBD, buildings are seen as strategic tools where strategic investments can yield important benefits. Yet to achieve these benefits, buildings must be planned, designed, and operated in a new way ... an EBD approach is a structured process that establishes broad agreement on the principles underlying a design, articulates goals that must be satisfied to achieve those principles, and sets measurable, expected outcomes (p. 7–8).

In addition, it is important to note that while the steps listed above appear linear, the EBD process itself is fluid. They are an integral part of the project, from its very inception through initial occupancy and the entire facility's lifecycle. Zimring et al (2008) continue, "[EBD] infuses these principles, goals, and expected outcomes throughout all steps of planning, designing, and operating buildings. It reflects an organization's ability to change, and a willingness to measure and confront the results of measurement" (p. 8).

As architects, designers, and healthcare administrators gain knowledge of the evidence-based design process, it also gains some criticism. In some cases, individuals argue that EBD is simply a 'buzzword'. If it is just a buzzword, Viets (2009) wonders, "how many people really practice it?" (p. 74). As more questions about the credibility of EBD arise, Viets (2009) finds it useful to draw comparisons to evidence-based medicine (EBM) in order to learn lessons to shape and understand the future of EBD.

"The field of medicine, like architecture, has faced many challenges in adopting an evidence-based approach. A number of these challenges are described [in Figure 3] ... "

"As EBM gained recognition, it faced a great deal of scrutiny ... [and] debates about EBM continue to this day" (Viets, 2009, p. 77). It is anticipated that "a lively debate about EBD" will continue.

> Comparing EBD to EBM, it is clear that EBD is in its youth. Less than a decade old, EBD stands to gain much from the evolution of its predecessor, EBM ... Architects should appreciate the high level of rigor associated with EBM and diligently strive to bring greater rigor to the field of EBD ... As healthcare architects educate themselves about the relationship between EBM and EBD, they will be better equipped to communicate with clients in the medical field and to follow the medical field's lead of transforming 'evidence-based' from a buzzword to an essential, value-adding part of their daily practice" (Viets, 2009, p. 86).

Figure 3:
Comparison of Evidence-Based Practices in Design and Medicine

Category of Comparison	Evidence-Based Medicine (EBM)	Evidence-Based Design (EBD)
First Formal Recognition	1992	2003
Types of Research Literature	Quantitative methods (including systematic reviews, meta-analyses, and randomized controlled trials) rank highest on the evidence pyramid.	Qualitative methods are common; quantitative methods are also used; few randomized controlled trials, systematic reviews, or meta-analyses.
Quantity of Literature Available	Huge and growing—more than 100,000 articles published worldwide in the top 50 biomedical journals from 1995—2002 (Soteriades, Rosmarakis, Paraschakis, & Falagas, 2006).	Relatively small, but growing body of rigorous studies relating to healthcare design (Ulrich et al, 2008).
Education	Research skills, methods, and concepts are ingrained in undergraduate and post-graduate education.	Limited but growing emphasis on research skills in design education.
Level of Rigor	Relatively high level of rigor in EBM because the education system teaches clinicians how to read, evaluate, and apply literature as well as how to conduct their own research.	Rigor is often misunderstood by designers. This may improve as the design community becomes more informed about EBD methods.

The EBD process requires an understanding of the healthcare delivery system, research, and the design and construction process. The remaining chapters cover this information in more detail.

The following is an example of how one healthcare organization addressed the healthcare trends and challenges discussed in this chapter by utilizing an EBD process.

Bronson Methodist Hospital, Kalamazoo, MI

The redevelopment of Bronson Methodist Hospital, which began in 1993, created a state-of-the-art, easily accessible healthcare campus that brings together inpatient care, outpatient care, and physician offices in a patient-focused healing environment.

Completed in 2000, this $210 million project, designed by Shepley, Bulfinch Richardson, and Abbott (located in Boston, MA), includes a medical office pavilion, an outpatient pavilion, and an inpatient pavilion that come together around a central garden atrium. Hamilton, Orr, and Raboin (2008) state that the design was based in part on evidence that positive distractions for patients and their families—such as art, music, and the influence of nature—play a positive supportive role in recovery.

Source: Reprinted with permission. (Bronson Methodist Hospital, North Pavilion and Bronson Methodist Hospital, 2010).

The project featured all private rooms, and the system's research showed hospital associated infections fell 11% (Nelson, 2006) resulting in an annual savings of $1.2 million. Bronson estimates it saves $500,000 a year in patient transfer costs. Other outcomes include 95.7% patient satisfaction (Rollins, 2004) and reduced nurse turnover (Nelson, 2006). Having grown by 40% since 2000, Bronson is currently using evidence-based design to develop a new inpatient pavilion for its birthing center and neonatal intensive care unit.

In March 2010, Bronson was named one of the nation's 100 Top Hospitals. This honor is based on results of the Thomson Reuters 100 Top Hospitals: National Benchmarks study. "Nearly 3,000 US hospitals were reviewed and the 100 Top Hospitals were selected based on objective statistical performance on Thomson Reuters' national balanced scorecard. The award recognized hospitals with the highest overall score across 10 areas: mortality, medical complications, patient safety, average length of stay, expenses, profitability, patient satisfaction, adherence to clinical standards of care, and post-discharge mortality and re-admission rates for acute myocardial infarction, heart failure, and pneumonia" (Bronson Methodist Hospital, 2010, para. 3). A Senior Vice President for Thomson Reuters explained that (as cited in Bronson Methodist Hospital, 2010, para. 6) "even during the economic downturn, the 100 Top Hospitals maintained a profit from operations while raising the bar for clinical quality and patient satisfaction." In the past, Bronson Methodist Hospital has received the following honors: "100 Top Hospitals: National Benchmarks (2005), 100 Top Hospitals: Performance Improvement Leader (2007), and 100 Top Hospitals: Cardiovascular Care (2008). These achievements combined with other national recognition such as the Malcolm Baldrige National Quality Award (2005), American Hospital Association-McKesson Quest for Quality Prize (2009), HealthGrades

Distinguished Hospital for Clinical Excellence (2009, 2010) and Magnet designation (2009), all add up to Bronson having the most consistently high-rated performance of any hospital in southwest Michigan" (Bronson Methodist Hospital, 2010, para. 7-8).

CHAPTER ONE REVIEW QUESTIONS

1. What are the seven current trends influencing healthcare in the United States today?
2. How can EBD positively influence the challenges represented by these trends?

NOTES

_____

_____

_____

_____

_____

_____

_____

_____

_____

_____

To check your answers see Appendix C

CHAPTER ONE QUIZ QUESTIONS

1. Select the best answer: Evidence-Based Design is the process of basing decisions about _____ on credible research to achieve the best possible outcomes.

    a. patient outcomes

    b. the built environment

    c. nursing staff to patient ratios

2. Which one of the following clinical and safety outcomes are typically NOT affected by the design of the physical healthcare environment?

    a. medical errors

    b. adverse reactions to drugs

    c. hospital-associated infections

3. The goal of the business case for EBD is to determine how healthcare facility investments contribute to improvements in patient care quality and the safety and satisfaction of both patients and staff while positively enhancing _____.

    a. the bottom line

    b. the physical design

    c. workforce efficiency

4. To make the business case for physical design innovations, what needs to be balanced against ongoing operating savings and revenue enhancements?

    a. patient outcomes

    b. one-time construction costs

    c. longer design and construction timelines

1) List and describe the various characteristics of healthcare settings in the US Healthcare Delivery System.

2) List the key stakeholders in healthcare facilities and describe the perspective each brings to the design of healthcare facilities.

3) Define and list the components of the Environment of Care (EOC).

Chapter Two at a Glance

Overview of the Healthcare Delivery System

■■ INTRODUCTION

One of the major strengths of the evidence-based design (EBD) process is that it values the expertise and perspectives of a variety of professionals, as well as the key stakeholders in the project. It encourages their involvement from the earliest point of the design project to maximize their input and cooperative problem-solving. However, bringing together this group of people (many of whom will form the backbone of the interdisciplinary team—the core group of people involved in the EBD process) means that professionals need to not only be well-versed in their primary professional focus (architecture, health administration, facilities planning, construction, research, clinical specialty, etc), but also that they have a clear overall understanding of the healthcare delivery system as it relates to specific projects.

Researchers, designers, equipment suppliers, and others interested in EBD must reach beyond their respective areas of expertise to recognize and value the relationship between what they do and the goals of the healthcare delivery system and its various member constituents. Being familiar with the basic concepts and challenges impacting the healthcare delivery system is critical for constituents to identify and implement potential solutions together that will positively affect the healthcare delivery system.

Every project is undertaken in a unique environment, which should be clearly understood prior to proceeding with the work. Evidence related to an outcome in one situation may not be directly transferable to another situation. A conscientious effort should be made prior to the work to understand and document the context within which the project is undertaken. Understanding the organization and its vision, mission, goals, leadership composition, team relationships, and organizational culture is necessary to achieve the best results for the healthcare project.

However, there are many types of healthcare facilities that make up the healthcare delivery system in the United States. Within this system, various types of facilities can be classified in a variety of ways.

This chapter gives an overview of the basic components of the healthcare delivery system by discussing facility types, based on their classifications as well as by the services. In addition, the following material further develops the context of the healthcare delivery system by discussing the key stakeholders and their roles in the healthcare facility and the EBD process.

The chapter explores how these key stakeholders influence the culture of the organization and how their buy-in is essential for the success of the EBD project, as they will become the champions for change.

■■ THE HEALTHCARE DELIVERY SYSTEM

Healthcare in the United States is predominately based on a medical model focused on diagnosis and treatment of illness. In the past few decades, a growing interest in a wellness model emphasizes health, disease prevention, and well-being (Austin & Wetle, 2008). A comprehensive definition of healthcare combines medical and wellness models and consists of the prevention, treatment, and management of illnesses and the preservation of mental and physical well-being.

Healthcare Settings and Characteristics

Healthcare delivery is basically a person-to-person interaction delivered within bricks-and-mortar facilities that house high-tech equipment, expert clinicians, and support staff (Garber, 2006). Healthcare is provided in different types of settings: inpatient hospitals, primary and outpatient care, and long-term-care settings.

Inpatient Hospitals

According to the American Hospital Association (AHA, 2007), a hospital is an institution with at least six beds whose primary function is to deliver patient services—diagnostic or therapeutic—for particular or general medical conditions. In addition, a hospital must be licensed, have an organized physician staff, and provide continuous nursing services under the supervision of registered nurses. The construction and operation of modern hospitals is governed by federal laws, state health department regulations, city ordinances, the standards of the Joint Commission, as well as national codes for building, fire protection, and sanitation.

Instead of a centralized system of hospitals under state ownership, there are a variety of institutional forms with both privately-owned and government-owned institutions under independent management. There is no simple classification. Hospitals are commonly classified in a few different ways, though these classifications are not mutually exclusive.

Classification by ownership

Public hospitals: Public hospitals are owned by federal, state, or local government agencies.

Federal hospitals: Federal hospitals are maintained primarily for specific groups of federal beneficiaries, such as Native Americans, military personnel, and veterans. Veterans Administration (VA) hospitals constitute the largest group of federally owned hospitals. As of 2008, the federal government owned and operated 213 hospitals (AHA, 2010). Local governments operate general public hospitals, 30% of which are located in large urban areas. These hospitals primarily serve indigent, minority, and inner-city populations.

Voluntary not-for-profit hospitals: Voluntary not-for-profit hospitals are privately owned hospitals operated on a not-for-profit, tax-exempt basis. Their primary mission is to benefit the community where they are located. The Internal Revenue Service Tax Code Section 501c3 grants tax-exempt status to organizations considered to be charitable (the promotion of health is considered to be a charitable activity) and operated for the public rather than private good (Gapenski, 2007). As of 2008, there were 2,923 nongovernment not-for-profit community hospitals (AHA, 2010).

Proprietary hospitals: For-profit, proprietary hospitals—also referred to as investor-owned hospitals—are owned by individuals, partnerships, or corporations. They are operated for the financial benefit of the entity that owns the institution—that is, the stockholders—and may declare dividends and distribute profits to individuals. They pay taxes just as other private corporations do (Griffith & White, 2007). As of 2008, 982 for-profit community hospitals were operational (AHA, 2010).

Public-Private Partnerships (P3)

It is important to note that healthcare facilities outside of the United States may be funded and managed differently. "In British Columbia, Canada, Public-private partnerships [P3s] have become significant in both social and infrastructure development. P3s exist in a variety of forms

---

[such as] the Canada Line rapid transit [and] the Abbotsford Regional Hospital and Cancer Centre (Wikipedia, en.wikipedia.org/wiki/Public–private_partnership, 2010)".

The P3 model is used internationally for major government funded projects including Canada, the United Kingdom, and Australia. The government (public) partners with a private sector consortium to design, build, and operate a building. The private sector partner is responsible for designing the building as per government specifications, constructing the building, and maintaining or operating the building for a fixed period of time. The government makes payments to the private sector for this service after the building is commissioned and turned over for occupancy. When the partnership contract period expires, the private sector consortium turns over the title of the building and the operational and maintenance duties to the government. This is similar to the "lease to own" concept in which payments are made for a fixed period of time, at the end of which, ownership is transferred. The contract can include any number of services to be provided by the private sector consortium including housekeeping, parking, and security, to name a few.

In Canada, typically a government funded major project requires a detailed business case which analyzes the life-cycle costs of several procurement options including the P3 model and traditional Design – Bid – Build. Life-cycle costs include one-time capital costs of building; ongoing operational and maintenance costs; the costs of major upgrades and rehabilitation; and costs associated with decommissioning or disposing the asset at the end of its useful life. The detailed business case compares the procurement models and makes a recommendation based on value.

A P3 must demonstrate that public interest will be served and value for money can be achieved. Public-private partnerships must provide some mix of the following benefits in order to deliver good value to government and citizens (Partnerships BC web site, 2010, www.partnershipsbc.ca).

- Timely Delivery: By taking advantage of private sector financing, government can build the needed infrastructure more quickly, avoiding up-front capital costs and paying for infrastructure over a fixed period of time after completion.
- Risk Transfer: The contractor, not the government, is liable for those costs associated with construction overruns and time delays. If contractors don't deliver, they don't get paid.
- Innovation: Private companies fully responsible for overruns have a greater incentive to innovate at every stage: through design, financing, construction methodology, and in operations and maintenance.

For example, for a new hospital procured using the P3 process, the government enters into an agreement with a private partner (private consortium) that designs, constructs, finances, maintains and operates the building for the life of the contract, all on a "for profit" basis. The government uses the hospital building to deliver its care, paying its private sector partner in regular installments for the life of the contract (for example, 30 years). At the end of this period, the hospital building ownership is transferred to the public owner who takes over the operating and maintenance functions. The private partner has fulfilled the contract and can move onto another project. In this way, the risk associated with project delivery/operations and maintenance is transferred to the P3 consortium until expiration of the contract (Partnerships BC website, www.partnershipsbc.ca). To fulfill the responsibilities of this undertaking, the consortium assembles a project team that brings together all of the expertise it will require to design and construct the building then operate and maintain it over the life of the contract (Watkinson, 2008). Typically, the team will include:

- financier (provides financial backing)
- contractor (responsible for construction of the building)
- design consultants (responsible for the design/construction of the building)
- operator (operates and maintains the building)

The EBD process is employed within a public-private partnership just as it is in a typical hospital build; however, because the public authority sets the guidelines and parameters of the performance specifications, it is best that evidence-based design principles are included as part of the performance specifications. The consortium may still employ the EBD principles; however they are not required to do so unless those principals are included in the specifications.

The EBD business case is strengthened within the P3 model when the contract sets out the terms for ongoing maintenance. A key player within the consortium—the maintenance partner or operator—has a vested interest in reducing long term maintenance costs, and will find value in employing the EBD process. The traditional challenge of balancing up-front capital costs against ongoing operational costs may be eased, because all P3 partners have a say in the project design and execution.

Classification by length of stay

Short-stay hospitals: Most hospitals are short-stay hospitals in which the average length of stay is less than 30 days. Patients admitted to short-stay hospitals suffer from acute conditions.

Long-term-care hospitals: Hospitals in which the length of stay exceeds 30 days are referred to as long-term-care hospitals. Such hospitals provide extended medical and rehabilitative care to patients with clinically complex acute and chronic conditions. As of 2008, Medicare had certified 129 long-term-care hospitals (AHA, 2010).

Classification by type of service

General acute-care hospitals: General acute-care hospitals provide a variety of services, including general and specialized medicine, general and specialized surgery, and obstetrics, to meet the general medical needs of the communities they serve. These hospitals provide diagnostic, treatment, and surgical services for patients with a variety of medical conditions. Most hospitals in the United States are general acute-care hospitals.

Specialty hospitals: Specialty hospitals admit only certain types and ages of patients or those with specified illnesses and conditions. Behavioral health or psychiatric hospitals provide diagnostic and treatment services for patients who have psychiatric-related illnesses; 447 specialty hospitals were operational as of 2008 (AHA, 2010). Rehabilitation hospitals specialize in providing restorative services to chronically ill and disabled individuals to a maximum level of functioning. Children's hospitals specialize in providing care to children from infancy through teen years. Some facilities deal with chronic and congenital conditions including cancer, cardiac, and orthopedic pediatric problems. There also are cancer, women's care, cardiac, surgical, and orthopedic specialty hospitals.

Classification by public access

Community hospitals: Community hospitals are nonfederal, short-stay, acute-care general or specialty hospitals whose facilities and services are available to the general public. In terms of ownership, community hospitals may be proprietary, voluntary, or owned by the state and local government. As of 2008, 5,010 community hospitals provided services in the United States (AHA, 2010).

Noncommunity hospitals: Noncommunity hospitals include hospitals operated by the federal government such as VA hospitals, prison hospitals, college infirmaries, and long-term-care hospitals.

Classification by location
Urban hospitals: Urban hospitals are defined as those located in a county that is part of a metropolitan statistical area (MSA)—a geographical area that includes at least one city with a population of 50,000 or more or an urbanized area of at least 50,000 inhabitants and a total population of 100,000. As of 2008, 3,012 urban community hospitals were operational (AHA, 2010).

Rural hospitals: Rural hospitals are located in a county that is not part of an MSA. As of 2008, 1,998 rural community hospitals were operational (AHA, 2010).

Classification by size
Classifying hospitals by size has not been standardized, but generally, they are viewed in the following manner:

- *small:* hospitals with fewer than 100 beds
- *medium:* hospitals with 100 to under 500 beds
- *large:* hospitals with more than 500 beds

Other Types of Hospitals
Teaching or academic hospitals: Teaching or academic hospitals are hospitals with approved residency programs for physicians. The presence of nursing programs or training affiliations for other health professionals, such as therapists and dietitians, does not make an institution a teaching hospital. Depending on the type and number of residency programs offered, a hospital is a minor or major teaching institution. To be a full teaching hospital, it should at a minimum provide residencies in general medicine, surgery, obstetrics and gynecology, and pediatrics.

Critical access-hospitals: Critical-access hospitals are rural limited-service hospitals that have been converted to the special designation of critical-access hospitals under the Medicare Rural Hospital Flexibility Program (a federal initiative). Most critical-access hospitals are in health-professional–shortage areas and/or medically underserved areas. Criteria in the program specify that the facility must be a not-for-profit or public hospital located more than 35 miles from any other hospital. The hospital must provide 24-hour emergency care services 7 days per week, and not have more than 15 acute-care inpatient beds. The hospital may have up to 10 additional swing beds that can be used interchangeably for acute or skilled nursing care, provided that not more than 15 beds are used at any one time for acute care.

Doctor-owned specialty hospitals: An 18-month ban by Congress on doctor-owned specialty hospitals was lifted in August 2006. Construction began on at least 30 doctor-owned hospitals in 2007. Critics of these facilities believe they skim the lucrative, highest-paying procedures and undercut not-for-profit community hospitals, which must continue to provide a wider array of costly services such as emergency and obstetrics departments, which increase the number of procedures performed in their specialty and drive up healthcare costs. Proponents believe they provide a new model for healthcare with higher quality care (Wall Street Journal, 2006).

Healthcare system: A healthcare system can have multiple hospitals that are owned, leased, sponsored, or contract managed by a central organization or a diversified single hospital system, according to the American Hospital Association (AHA, 2010). As of 2008, 2,868 community hospitals were members of a healthcare system.

Healthcare network: A healthcare network is a group of hospitals, physicians, other providers, insurers, and/or community agencies that work together to provide a broad complement of services to their constituents (AHA, 2010). As of 2008, 1,490 community hospitals were members of a healthcare network.

Primary and Outpatient Care Services

Primary care: Primary care is regarded as essential healthcare. As such, the goal of the healthcare delivery system is to optimize population health, not just the health of individuals who have the means to access health services. Primary care is the first contact a patient makes with the healthcare delivery system. The primary care practitioner tends to serve as the gatekeeper for the system. One of the main functions of primary care is to coordinate the delivery of healthcare services between the patient and the myriad components of the delivery system.

Ambulatory Care: Weill Cornell

Completed in January 2007, the 13-story, $230 million state-of-the-art ambulatory-care and medical-education building was designed to enhance the patient experience in every way. This facility offers a number of special amenities, including the Patient Welcome Resource Center, a spacious and comfortable area for patients and families to rest between appointments, as well as an array of medical information and assistance with medical billing and insurance questions. Consolidating key clinical programs in one location also makes it easier for patients to access services and care under one roof.

The new building, designed by Polshek Partnership and Ballinger, features architectural elements geared toward maximizing an atmosphere of wellness and comfort: reflecting pools and cascading water features, large picture windows that allow for natural light, and design features and colors that add to a soothing environment.

Together with Cornell University's Department of Environmental Design and Analysis, the Weill Cornell Medical College's Physician Organization is conducting several research projects in conjunction with the development of a new ambulatory care building and the introduction of its Weill Cornell: We Care Program to enhance the patient experience. The Physician Organization is the faculty practice of Weill Cornell's more than 700 physician/teachers. Included in its studies are whether the introduction of an electronic medical record enhances physician-to-physician communication and if that enhances patient satisfaction; whether the use of patient educational information as part of the visit enhances patient satisfaction; and if there is a statistical relationship between the attractiveness of an environment and patients' perceptions of various components of their visit.

Upon opening the building, a study of the patient check-in and check-out process in the new locations (featuring operational changes and new design features expected to reduce patient time) will be conducted to measure against the existing processes that do not include the new design features. Preliminary studies in six existing ambulatory sites found:

- The more attractive the environment, the higher the perceived quality and the lower the anxiety.
- Patients underestimated longer (30+ minutes) actual wait times and overestimated short (0-5 minutes) actual wait times.
- No significant relationship existed between actual wait times and perceived quality or perceived anxiety.
- Significant relationship between perceived wait times and perceived quality and perceived anxiety (Becker & Douglas, 2008).

Outpatient services: Outpatient services are also referred to as ambulatory care. Strictly speaking, ambulatory care constitutes diagnostic and therapeutic services and treatments provided to the walking (ambulatory) patient (AHA, 2007). Hence, in a restricted sense, ambulatory care refers to care rendered to patients who come to physicians' offices, outpatient departments of hospitals, and health centers to receive care. Outpatient services are not provided on the basis of an overnight stay in which room and board costs are incurred.

The various settings in which outpatient service delivery are found in the US healthcare delivery system can be grouped as follows:

- private practice
- hospital-based outpatient services
- freestanding facilities
- mobile medical
- diagnostic and screening services
- home health services
- hospice services
- ambulatory long-term care services
- public health services
- public and voluntary clinics
- telephone access
- telemedicine
- wellness centers
- complementary alternative care medicine

Private practice: Physicians, as office-based professionals, form the backbone of ambulatory care and constitute the majority of primary care services. Most patient visits entail relatively limited examination and testing, and encounters with the physician are generally relatively quick. Apart from physicians, other private professionals often work in solo or group practice, for example, dentists, optometrists, podiatrists, psychologists, and physical, occupational, and speech therapists.

Medical homes: The medical home is a relatively new concept for providing comprehensive primary care through stronger partnerships with physicians and patients. Patient-centered medical homes feature physicians responsible for whole person care; care management is provided electronically and with open scheduling, expanded hours, and group visits across the health system and community.

Alternative care models: "New models of care are emerging as traditional care gives way to alternatives outside of physicians' offices and hospitals…[there is an expected] increase in the number and scope of services offered by work site, retail health clinics, and home health services, and a broader approach to the definition of healthcare environments" (Zensius, 2010, p. 32).

Hospital-Based Outpatient Services

Hospital-based outpatient services can be broadly classified into five main types: clinical, surgical, emergency, home health, and women's health. Outpatient services now constitute a key source of profit for hospitals; hospitals have expanded their outpatient departments and utilization has grown.

Clinical services: Clinical services correspond to services provided by private physicians in their offices.

Surgical services: Hospital-based ambulatory surgery centers provide same-day surgical care, and patients are discharged after a few hours of recovery following surgery.

Emergency services: More than 90% of all community hospitals in the United States provide emergency services. The main purpose of this department is to have services available around the clock for patients who are acutely ill or injured, particularly those with serious or life-threatening conditions requiring immediate attention.

Home healthcare: Home health departments in hospitals provide post-acute care and rehabilitation therapies.

Women's health centers: Women's health centers specialize in meeting the healthcare needs of women.

Freestanding Facilities

Freestanding facilities are known by different names: walk-in clinics, surgicenters, emergicenters, and urgent care centers. These facilities have given patients a wider range of healthcare choices and attempt to meet consumer needs of convenience and cost reduction. These clinics are often owned or controlled by corporations and/or physicians.

Walk-in clinics: Walk-in clinics provide basic primary care to urgent care, but they are generally used on a nonroutine, episodic basis.

Urgent care centers and emergicenters: Urgent care centers and emergicenters are open 24 hours a day, 7 days a week, and accept patients with no appointments. They provide a wide range of routine services for basic and acute conditions on a first-come, first-serve basis.

Surgicenters: Surgicenters are freestanding ambulatory surgery centers often independent of hospitals. They provide a full range of services for the types of surgery that can be performed on an outpatient basis and do not require hospitalization.

Mobile, medical, diagnostic, and screening services: Mobile, medical, diagnostic, and screening services are healthcare services transported to patients. Routine health service such as eye care and dental care can also be brought to patients. Mobile diagnostic services include mammography and magnetic resonance imaging.

Safety Net

The definition of safety net has been widely debated. The Institute of Medicine (IOM) defines the safety net as, "those providers that organize and deliver a significant level of health care and other health-related services to uninsured, Medicaid, and other vulnerable patients" (Institute of Medicine, 2000). Much of the discussion focuses on which providers in a community are safety net providers, and which ones are not. The IOM also recognized the concept of core safety net providers: "These providers have two distinguishing characteristics: (1) by legal mandate or explicitly adopted mission they maintain an 'open door', offering access to services to patients regardless of their ability to pay; and (2) a substantial share of their patient mix is uninsured, Medicaid, and other vulnerable patients" (Institute of Medicine 2000).

Some core safety net providers include health centers (such as, Community Health Centers, Migrant Health Centers, the Health Care for the Homeless Program, School-Based Health Centers, and the Public Health Housing Program), and public and teaching hospitals as well as care provided in hospital emergency departments and private physicians offices (Oregon State Web Site, 2010).

Long-Term-Care Services

Long-term care refers to any personal care or assistance that a patient receives on an ongoing basis because of a disability or chronic illness that limits his or her ability to function. Long-term care may be provided in a range of settings such as an individual's home or residential, assisted living, nursing-care, or rehabilitation facilities. In some settings, individuals may spend short periods of time (90 days or less) for rehabilitation before returning to the community. In other settings, individuals stay much longer, often through their last days.

The term *resident* rather than *patient* is more commonly used when referring to individuals residing in long-term care settings. Most individuals receiving long-term care suffer from some chronic illness and the focus of care is usually on supporting and maintaining their health status rather than curing. While all different types of individuals (young and old) might use long-term care services, the overall usage of long-term-care services and products is highest among older adults. Long-term care for older

> The prevalence of chronic conditions is projected to increase dramatically with the aging of the population. In fact, by the year 2030, nearly 150 million Americans will have a chronic condition. Consequently, the need for quality long-term care will also increase in the years to come (Shi & Singh, 2001).

adults is provided in a range of community-based settings, such as the individual's home, adult daycare, and senior centers.

Institutional long-term care: Institutional long-term care is provided to individuals whose needs cannot be met in a less acute, community-based setting. A continuum of services can be provided through different long-term care settings based on the individual's acuity (the intensity of care necessary to meet the needs of a patient) level and dependency. Available options for long-term care along the continuum of care include independent or retirement living centers, assisted living facilities, and skilled nursing facilities or nursing homes.

Independent living: Independent living centers are often referred to as retirement communities, congregate living, or senior apartments and are designed specifically for independent senior adults who are able to live on their own but desire the security and conveniences of community living. Some communities offer organized social and recreational activities (congregate living and retirement communities), while others provide housing with only a minimal amount of amenities and services (senior apartments). There are no health services provided by the organization, but many communities allow the resident to pay for a home health aide or nurse to come and assist with medicines and personal care. These types of housing units are residential in character.

Assisted living: An assisted living facility is defined as "a long-term care alternative that involves the delivery of professionally managed personal and healthcare services in a group setting that is residential in character and appearance in ways that optimizes the physical and psychological independence of residents" (Regnier, 1994). Although the main component of assisted living involves help with activities of daily living, the overall philosophy is one of personal self-management. These facilities do not provide skilled nursing care. They are known by different names in different parts of the United States: board and care, residential care, community-based retirement care, personal care, adult living, or adult foster care facilities.

Nursing homes: Nursing homes or skilled nursing facilities are designed for seniors who are in need of 24-hour nursing care. Nursing facilities provide many of the same residential components of other senior-care options including room and board, personal care, and protection-supervision and may offer other types of therapy. Their onsite clinical staff sets them apart from other types of senior housing. Regulations specify the staff-to-patient ratios as well as the location of the nurses' station to monitor patients. Nursing homes have been modeled physically and operationally around the hospital, but recent innovations strive to achieve residential settings and operations that support resident's preferred routines as well as their physical and cognitive needs.

Continuing care retirement communities: Continuing care retirement communities (CCRCs) are residential campuses that provide a continuum of care, from private units to assisted living and skilled nursing care, all in one location. CCRCs are designed to offer active seniors an independent lifestyle from the privacy of their home but also include the availability of services in an assisted living environment and onsite intermediate or skilled nursing care, if necessary.

Alzheimer disease/dementia care: Although many assisted living communities and nursing homes cater to individuals with Alzheimer disease and other related memory disorders or dementia, the trend is toward facilities that provide specialized care and housing tailored to the special needs of individuals with this disease. These facilities offer care that fosters residents' individual skills and interests in an environment that helps diminish confusion and agitation. Most of these facilities provide assistance with bathing, grooming, dressing, and other daily activities.

Despite the wide range of facilities and patient populations they serve, one thing all healthcare organizations have in common is they have key stakeholders—people who have a vested interest in the success or failure of the built environment and organizational culture.

▪▪ KEY STAKEHOLDERS AND THE INTERDISCIPLINARY PROJECT TEAM

It's important to the success of the EBD process to get buy-in from key stakeholders as well as their input throughout the project to ensure that all the stakeholders' needs and perspectives are considered. In fact, these stakeholders are often the same people who will form the backbone of the interdisciplinary team—the core group of people who will envision, champion, create, innovate, implement, and design the EBD process for each individual project.

Therefore, understanding each type of stakeholder is essential for the individual practicing evidence-based design. Depending on the project, they can include but are not limited to:

- board of trustees and leadership
- researchers and designers
- vendors/suppliers
- patients
- caregivers/family/visitors
- staff
- community partners
- community organizations
- donors

Board of Trustees and Leadership

For-profit, nonprofit, and governmental boards exist in healthcare environments, depending on whether the type of healthcare facility is investor-owned, not-for-profit community-based, or operated by a government agency. Those boards are ultimately accountable for organizational activity, accomplishment, and major capital investments. They differ in the amount of public scrutiny they receive, the degree to which procedures of governance must be adhered to by law, and the strength of the traditions and culture that drive their practices.

For-profit or investor-owned boards: For-profit or investor-owned boards run healthcare business corporations that are obligated to produce a return for stockholders.

Not-for-profit boards: Not-for-profit boards run healthcare corporations that are chartered for a charitable purpose with no stock ownership and are exempt from certain taxes.

Governmental boards: Governmental boards often have elected officials and more legal requirements regarding board composition and process than either profit or not-for-profit boards. They may or may not have taxing authority.

Good board governance focuses on establishing and supporting a vision and values for the organization; maintaining an external, future-oriented, and proactive focus; enabling an outcome-driven organizing system that stays focused on the big issues; facilitating diversity and unity; and balancing over and under control with executive management (Carver, 2006).

One of the most important functions of a board is to select the chief executive officer (CEO). The CEO of the healthcare organization is also a member of the board, most often with voting rights. As such, the CEO is a key decision maker who aids the board in creating a future vision for the organization, which may include a building project. The most effective relationship occurs when the board attends to its responsibilities and the CEO to his or hers, with appropriate interaction. While an entire staff is required to do the organization's work, the board is best able to maintain its big picture focus by interacting with the CEO.

The CEO is accountable for all services and behaviors of the organization; in fact, the CEO is responsible for everything but the board and its functions. He or she is accountable to the board as a whole and receives his or her annual performance review from the board based on the overall performance of the organization. To assure maximum success for the organization, all component parts including the board, CEO, staff, and the relationships amongst the various parts must be strong and effective (Carver, 2006).

Members of the senior management team in a healthcare organization include chiefs or vice presidents (Figure 4). These members may include the chief operating officer, finance officer, nursing officer, medical officer, and other key positions dictated by needs such as information systems, development (fundraising), business development, marketing, etc. The levels of management hierarchy begin with senior managers who select midlevel managers who, in turn, select first-line supervisors to carry out daily operational duties. The management team works with staff, physicians, patients, and family members to carry out the mission of the organization.

In healthcare boards, there is a third power—relationships with physicians. The board grants privileges to physicians to practice in the hospital. Physicians granted such privileges constitute an organized body called the medical staff, which does not work for the board unless they are employed physicians. Often, the medical staff is directly represented on the board.

Healthcare systems can have differing board structures. Some have only one board for the entire healthcare system, while others maintain a community board for each hospital that reports into an overarching board for the system (Figure 4).

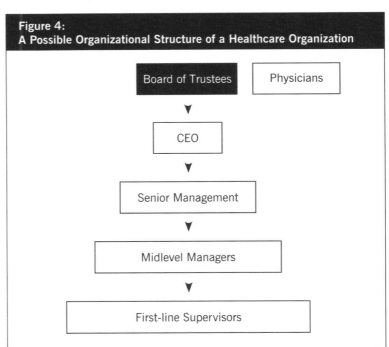

Figure 4:
A Possible Organizational Structure of a Healthcare Organization

Building a new facility or embarking upon a major renovation is a strategic policy decision made by the board that requires careful analysis of community needs and ability to fund the endeavor. It is generally a major capital expense included in strategic master facility plans created to meet future needs for expansion or improvements. The board of trustees ultimately has authority for building decisions of this magnitude. The board and other facility leaders have a critical role to play to ensure the successful implementation of the EBD process.

In the case of healthcare construction, the CEO recommends to the board, based upon detailed information and analysis from senior staff, that millions of dollars should be spent that will further enable the healthcare facility to meet community needs and/or shareholder value. The board approves or disapproves the recommendation. Any major change in cost, shape, scope, or timing of the project must be taken back to the board for further approval.

The senior management team and other key managers appointed by the CEO, such as the facilities manager, often serve as voting or nonvoting members of the building steering committee for the building project. They are responsible for researching and recommending actions based on their technical knowledge and the clinical and support needs of patients, families, and staff.

Researchers and Designers

Researchers assist in the initial development of project goals and accompanying hypotheses to frame a study. As the interdisciplinary team develops ideas, the researcher can assist in searching for relevant evidence. This participation ensures that the research process, when completed, can be presented as valid.

A research team (or single researcher) may include individuals with research degrees, students, or those with experience, particularly in research related to the built environment. In addition, other key members of a research team may include the hospital's quality improvement, records, finance, and information systems managers, as well as other clinicians who will aid in identifying, tracking, and monitoring clinical and financial indicators significant to the project goals.

Interdisciplinary project team members will work together as participants when executing the key steps of the EBD process:

- Define evidence-based goals and objectives.
- Find sources for relevant evidence.
- Critically interpret relevant evidence.
- Create and innovate evidence-based design concepts.
- Develop a hypothesis.
- Collect baseline performance measures.
- Monitor implementation of design and construction.
- Measure post-occupancy performance results.

The teams of professionals vary depending on skills required to meet the challenge at each phase of the project, such as visioning, strategic planning, functional programming, preconceptual design, conceptual design, schematic design, design development, construction documents, construction administration, commissioning, and post-occupancy evaluation. They bring the knowledge of their primary focus to bear on the identified challenge (The Center for Health Design, 2007).

Patients

Today's consumer-oriented culture mandates that leaders consider the wants as well as needs of the ultimate consumer. In healthcare, this is the person seeking healthcare services, referred to here as the patient. (The term *resident*, rather than *patient*, is more commonly used when referring to individuals residing in long-term care settings.) Competitive forces place a great emphasis on patient satisfaction results for many healthcare organizations. Patient satisfaction surveys are often oriented to facility amenities and staff behaviors during a healthcare interaction, as opposed to the actual evaluation of quality of care or care outcomes.

According to Stone (2008), "Patients and their families have described a more patient-centered approach as key to meeting their needs. Characteristics of the desired model include: respect for patients, coordination of care, patient education, physical comfort, emotional support, and involvement of family and friends" (p. 56).

Vendors

Just as other professionals can bring another perspective to the project (and the interdisciplinary team), so can vendors. Integrating these professionals into the team early in the design process means they can support opportunities for more flexible spaces with such considerations as acoustics, sustainability practices, materials selection, wayfinding, and a possible reduction in the overall space requirements.

Knowledgeable vendors can share considerable product and trend information as well as future product development plans, eliminating the issue of potentially selecting outdated products. (This occurs as selections are made, in some cases, years before move in.) Some suppliers may even house their own research team which, when partnered with the design professionals, can together investigate challenges within the environment and solutions that may not have otherwise been discovered. Additionally, vendors, in partnership with the design firm and researchers, can often share lessons learned from other healthcare facilities with similar challenges and work closely with the design team to:

- validate the design challenges
- participate with the interdisciplinary team in creating design solutions
- provide best practices on how to implement proposed new design concepts

The key is to create a comprehensive list of vendors and make selections early based on the qualifications of the company and its dedication to the EBD process. Once the interdisciplinary team is in place, their expertise can help create spaces that fulfill the vision.

Amenities are often included in studies of patient perceptions of the care experience (for example, comfort, security, cleanliness, ease of access, and visual and auditory privacy) and should be considered in the early phases of planning. It is important to understand that selected amenities can impact future patient perceptions of care when surveys are conducted.

**Patient-Centered Care: The Children's Hospital at Fitzsimons
in Aurora, Colorado**

After five years of careful planning, generous donations, and hard work, the new Children's Hospital in Aurora, Colorado, opened its doors on September 29, 2007. As a private, not-for-profit pediatric healthcare network, The Children's Hospital is 100% dedicated to caring for children of all ages and stages of growth.

This replacement facility reflects The Children's Hospital's commitment to providing the most advanced, state-of-the-art healthcare in the country. The Children's Hospital is located on 48 acres of land on the southern edge of the University of Colorado Health Sciences Center Campus at Fitzsimons in Aurora. The new $450 million Children's Hospital is a nine-story, freestanding facility of approximately 900,000 square feet. It is 73% larger than the previous facility and houses 270 beds and more than 2,000 parking spaces. Connected to the new inpatient hospital is a faculty office building, an ambulatory building, and pavilion to create a facility that contains a total of 1.4 million square feet. The design team is a collaboration of ZGF Architects and H+L Architecture.

The Children's Hospital features all private patient rooms with accommodations for family members. The hospital also offers increased family-based amenities, such as family lounges, additional sleep rooms, family library and business center, and expanded sibling childcare. Additionally, patient portals are available in patient rooms through which patients and families may view local television, cable programming, and video-on-demand. Every aspect of the hospital was developed with the best interest of the patients and their families in mind. The hospital has critical adjacencies (units grouped together for maximum efficiency) designed into the facility.

Caregivers, Family, and Visitors

Parallel with patient satisfaction concerns are the needs of visitors to the health facility. Most patients are accompanied, or visited, by one or more persons during their healthcare interaction. An inpatient stay can greatly elevate the number of persons interfacing with the facility as patient visitors. As the aging population increases, the number of visitors with motor, auditory, or visual impairments, along with cardiac and pulmonary insufficiencies, will require special facility accommodations. Therefore, consideration of family and visitor needs as part of the EBD process is likely to result in a more patient- and family-centered environment and increased patient satisfaction.

Staff

Participative management—a management style that encourages employees to have a strong decision-making role—came into the mainstream of acceptance in the early 1980s. However, Hickey and Casner-Lotto (1998) state that "only recently has a significant number of organizations recognized that broad, systematic participation is the most effective way to tap work-force knowledge" (p. 58). It has taken more than 20 years for this concept to infiltrate healthcare design planning.

The strength of participative management is in getting those at the staff-client interface to be involved in key decisions. Purser and Cabana (1997) state, "Planning in fast-paced environments requires continuous organizational learning. For this to happen, organizations must function as open systems capable of responding to trends within and between their systems and environment. Strategies that yield success in the future will be those that are created by the employees and for the customer" (p. 66).

Participative Team Approach: Palomar Pomerado Health System in Poway and Escondido, California

When Palomar Pomerado Health System needed to build a replacement facility, leadership realized the need for a participatory team design approach.

The plan for the construction of a replacement facility utilized a participatory evidence-based design process that included individuals from all departments within the hospital. The goal was to modify the design process to facilitate greater involvement and participation from staff with the intent that the participants would play an active role in creating and disseminating knowledge about the design throughout the organization. Champion teams were created and served as think tanks to identify, evaluate, and challenge innovative design concepts. These teams were also meant to serve as resources to the user groups and steering committee.

Palomar Pomerado Health System joined The Center for Health Design's Pebble Project™ research initiative and, along with the help of Georgia Institute of Technology, documented the process and identified lessons learned. Interviews, along with focus groups, were conducted by researchers from CHD and Georgia Tech, and several benefits of the process emerged. These included effects on staff behavior, attitude, and culture; acceptance of innovative design concepts; deeper facility-wide understanding of the benefits of design innovations; and broader communication and dissemination of ideas. Additionally, this became a model for future participatory processes where high staff input and participation are desirable.

For additional information on Palomar Pomerado's project, see Guide 2: Building the Evidence Base.

Participative management strategies applied to facility design call for staff involvement to design effective and efficient facilities. In addition to clinical staff, other employees, such as those from housekeeping and information technology, can also provide invaluable insights into all aspects of design. For example, housekeeping staff are intimately aware of what colors and textures show dirt easily and wear prematurely, while clinical staff can provide feedback about the layout of supply and equipment spaces, work-surface heights and locations, as well as actual care provision areas. IT staff can help forecast space requirements for future equipment needs.

Current best practice includes providing mockups at various stages of development for staff to evaluate for efficiency. Mockups provide the ability to perform failure mode analysis in the simulated work environment. Mockups ideally include not only a patient room, which has been the traditional mockup scenario, but also the staff work area if possible. It is important to outfit the final phase of the mockup with the equipment planned for the new facility. Often vendors will provide equipment for the mockups. Virtual mockups provide an initial means to consider three-dimensional spaces. Full-scale virtual mockups in virtual-reality caves provide an emerging means for clients to visualize spaces and functions.

Community Partners

Involvement of community partners such as paramedical, law enforcement, funeral home, and area church staff can be crucial to a positively viewed design by these significant partners in care. The influence of these partners on community sentiment is immeasurable. Involving other public officials may be important to the acceptance of the design plans in the community to the extent there are no ethical, legal, or political impediments to this involvement. Getting community input and support for the project—their buy-in—will inform the design, ensure that the project considers the needs of these constituents, and perhaps, most importantly, enlists their help in promoting the project.

Community Organizations

Many associations exist to provide expert advice for the care of their constituencies. For example, the National Association of the Deaf (NAD) is available to consult on interventions that assist in accommodating the needs of the hearing impaired. In addition to constituency organizations, public institutions such as libraries, historical societies, and disaster committees can provide important information to a healthcare facility in a number of ways that can benefit facility design.

Donors

For not-for-profit organizations, fundraising is often the means of funding a new facility. Most donors have some type of relationship with their donor facility, such as being a past patient or family member of a patient; asking them to participate in the design process of a new project strengthens this existing relationship. This not only will make it more likely that they will continue to provide financial support to the organization, but also that they will become champions of the initiative and encourage even more donations and good will from the community.

Inclusion and buy-in of stakeholders is essential for a successful EBD process. Key stakeholders can influence the culture of an organization or project or even change it. According to Hamilton et al (2008), "true transformation will occur only when programs are integrated into the very fabric of an organization" (p. 54).

One of the most obvious cultural artifacts is the physical environment of the organization (Hamilton & Orr, 2006). The physical environment continuously sends out messages about the organization to all who encounter it. The environment influences behaviors of those who experience it (Gifford, 1997). For this reason, design of the environment powerfully impacts culture.

- The physical environment can serve as an enabler or barrier to desired behaviors.
- Deliberate design of the environment thus becomes an important variable in the design of desired organizational cultures.

ORGANIZATIONAL CULTURE AND CHANGE IN HEALTHCARE

Culture is defined as a powerful set of norms, habits, policies, procedures, artifacts, symbols, and rituals that govern behavior in an organization or, simply stated, the atmosphere and character of an organization (Schein, 1992). Smart leaders recognize that their most valuable assets are people and culture. It is widely known that organizations that establish a particular culture will be superior in practice to those who forsake culture for strategy; culture will win every time.

Can the components of culture be used to unleash the ability to innovate and show compassion and care within a facility? The Environment of Care (EOC) is based on the understanding that the experience a person has in a healthcare delivery system is a function of the six components that define the EOC. The impact of the physical environment on organizational culture can be expressed through the EOC. It is also the context within which an EBD process occurs (American Institute of Architects, 2006).

The six components of the EOC target the areas in which the physical environment can serve as an enabler or barrier to desired behaviors. Deliberate design of the environment becomes an important variable in creating a desired organizational culture (The relationship between these components will be discussed in *Guide 3: Integrating Evidence-Based Design*.)

The six components that define the EOC are:

- delivery of care model (concepts)
- facility and service users (people)
- systems design
- layout and operational planning
- physical environment
- design process and implementation

An understanding of the EOC can be applied to the entire healthcare system, to the design of a healthcare facility, or to a single aspect of an existing facility; no matter the type or size of the facility or system, all of the components of the EOC are present. These components define the culture of these organizations. Individuals practicing evidence-based design understand that the physical environment is only one of the components of the EOC; however, it is the relationship between all of the components that impact culture and enhance the EBD process. Understanding the relationship between them allows individuals to identify the design strategies that will yield the greatest outcomes. (For more information on the Environment of Care, *see Guide 3: Integrating Evidence-Based Design*.)

Having an awareness of the interaction and relationship of the EOC components will help individuals practicing evidence-based design understand that every healthcare organization has a unique culture which needs to be considered and addressed during the EBD process. Based on deep underlying assumption and shared beliefs, much of what constitutes culture is unstated (Schein, 1992).

Culture in an organization is shaped by stated and unstated values, the shared assumptions of its members, its policies and procedures, and its official and informal organizational structures, along with the various observed symbols and artifacts (Schein,

---

2010 *Guidelines for the Design and Construction of Health Care Facilities*

The 2010 Edition of the Facilities Guidelines Institute (FGI) *Guidelines for the Design and Construction of Health Care Facilities* combines two formerly separate chapters. "Chapters 1.2 (Environment of Care) and 1.5 (Planning, Design, and Construction) from the 2006 edition have been combined into a new Chapter 1.2 (Planning, Design, Construction, and Commissioning)" (Facilities Guidelines Institute, 2010, p. xxv). In addition, information on the functional program for the Environment of Care includes expanded "text on projected operational use and demand on short- and long-term planning considerations" (FGI, p. xxv). The EOC components described here are the same as the first edition study guides.

2004). While the mission and vision may be visible, the observed actions and behaviors of individuals within the organization may indicate an entirely different set of values (Schein, 1992).

Organizational culture is not monolithic. While the overarching culture of the organization guides much of organizational behavior, subcultures exist within most organizations, especially complex ones like healthcare systems (Schein, 2004; Kotter & Heskett, 1992). Organizational culture in healthcare has evolved into several identifiable models, including examples such as:

- cultures of safety
- faith-based cultures of caring
- patient- and family-centered cultures
- physician-centered cultures
- profit-minded corporate cultures
- bureaucratic and hierarchical cultures
- academic and research cultures

Awareness of the attributes that will contribute to positive organizational change and culture is essential for a successful EBD process and project. It is possible, although extremely difficult, to transform organizational culture to a desired model (Schein, 2004). Culture, because it is so deep-rooted in the organization, has a tendency to return to the previous state.

However, based on the concepts of sociotechnical theory, culture change initiatives are more likely to stick when they combine simultaneous interventions to both the social and technical aspects of the organization (Appelbaum, 1997). Cultural transformation is, therefore, more likely to succeed if there is a coordinated attempt to jointly optimize culture change and facility design. This joint optimization will involve every component of the healthcare organization.

Change and innovation often fail not because the ideas were inappropriate but rather the organization could not bring about or sustain the required change (Caldwell et al., 2008). The role of leadership in organizational change, particularly transformational change, is an important element. When the leader is involved and committed to the strategy, success is more likely to occur. Transformational change is a co-creation through the efforts of many people, all performing their specific role and function in the best manner possible. The leadership capacity must be expanded beyond the CEO and senior leaders into work groups, teams, and all stakeholders for maximum change to occur. Often there is a passionate integrator within the organization that is seen by their peers as a leader. By involving this person on your project team, chances of success improve.

The EBD process is successful in achieving its goals if it is considered in conjunction with a range of different factors. The EBD process alone is not sufficient to make improvements in the physical environment. Referenced here is a 2008 model created by Craig Zimring, Godfried M. Augenbroe, Eileen Malone, and Blair Sadler that provides a framework for understanding how the physical environment interacts with a range of different factors in achieving desired outcomes:

> Harnessing EBD as a transformational force and tool requires system-wide implementation to ensure meaningful implementation across clinical and business processes; it also entails the ability to articulate clearly the value of a given capital investment across its lifecycle. The key variable has been and always will be – leadership. Well conceived strategies fail without transformational leaders and disciplined execution (Casscells, Kurmel, Ponatoski, 2009, p. 140).

This conceptual framework (Figure 5) demonstrates how EBD supports the creation of a healing environment to improve outcomes through an internal synergy of efforts between leaders, transforming culture with re-engineered clinical and administrative processes and infrastructure investments. The best research-generated evidence should be used to implement a focused plan, all of which is dynamically shaped by external forces.

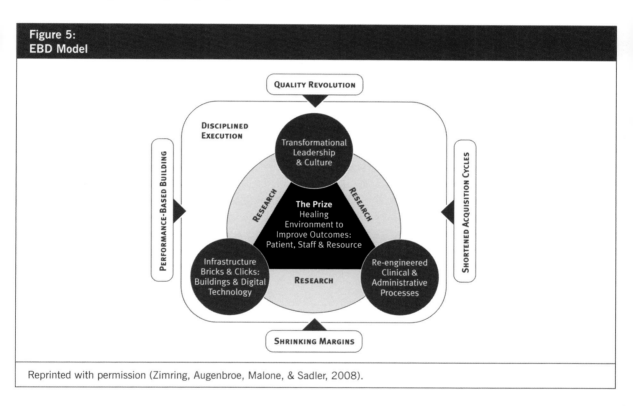

Figure 5:
EBD Model

Reprinted with permission (Zimring, Augenbroe, Malone, & Sadler, 2008).

There is great potential for transformational change within a health-care organization that has the opportunity to design a new facility. The opportunity afforded by new construction can significantly impact the ability of organizations and caregivers to provide safer, high-quality, more-efficient, and satisfying healthcare services, as well as new programs and technology for their communities.

CHAPTER TWO REVIEW QUESTIONS

1. What are the six typical classifications for inpatient hospitals?
2. What are five other types of inpatient hospitals?
3. Name three types of hospital-based outpatient services.
4. Name two types of free-standing facilities.
5. List the nine key stakeholders in healthcare facilities.
6. Why is it important to consider the perspective(s) of hospital staff when designing a healthcare facility?
7. Why is it important to consider the perspective(s) of community-based organizations or associations in the design of a healthcare facility?
8. Which professionals might comprise a hospital design research team?
9. What are the six components that make up the Environment of Care (EOC)?

NOTES

To check your answers see Appendix C

CHAPTER TWO QUIZ QUESTIONS

1. Facilities that give patients a wide range of healthcare choices and attempt to meet consumer needs of convenience and cost reduction are collectively known as _____.
   a. walk-in clinics
   b. surgicenters
   c. freestanding facilities

2. _____ refers to any personal care or assistance that a patient receives on an ongoing basis because of a disability or chronic illness that limits his or her ability to function.
   a. Long-term care
   b. Institutional care
   c. Home health care

3. Hospital-based outpatient services can be broadly classified into five main types: clinical, surgical, emergency, home health, and _____ health.
   a. psychiatric
   b. women's
   c. pediatric

4. Outpatient services are also referred to as _____ care.
   a. ambulatory
   b. walk-in
   c. non-institutional

5. Preliminary studies by the Weill Cornell Medical College's Physician Organization in six existing ambulatory sites found that the more attractive the environment, the _____ the perceived quality and the _____ the anxiety.
   a. higher, higher
   b. lower, lower
   c. higher, lower

6. Hospital boards are ultimately accountable for organizational activity, accomplishment, and _____.

   a. staff satisfaction

   b. patient outcomes

   c. major capital investments

7. Who is accountable for all of the services and behaviors of a hospital's organization?

   a. the board chair

   b. the entire board

   c. the CEO

8. Who recommends expenditures to further enable the healthcare facility to meet community needs and/or shareholder value? Who approve(s) or disapprove(s) the recommendation?

   a. board, CEO

   b. CEO, board

   c. CEO, government

9. Which strategy applied to facility design calls for staff involvement in the design of effective and efficient facilities based on their day-to-day experience?

   a. total quality management

   b. universal design management

   c. participative management

10. A facility's Environment of Care is defined by its _____:

    a. physical design

    b. culture

    c. outcomes

Define *research*
in the context of
Evidence-Based Design.

Identify sources for relevant
evidence within the
healthcare facility itself and
how they can be used.

Identify several ways in
which research can be used
to improve outcomes.

Chapter Three at a Glance

Introduction to Research

3 Chapter Three

■■ INTRODUCTION

Evidence-based design (EBD) is the process of basing decisions about the built environment on credible research to achieve the best possible outcomes (The Center for Health Design, 2008b). This process begins with identifying the vision and key overall goals and objectives for the project. It is the role of the interdisciplinary team to determine how these goals will be achieved through the selection of design strategies along with the integration of technology, cultural transformation, and re-engineered care and business processes.

EBD is value-driven in the sense that the organization wants to significantly improve healthcare quality, safety, and patient- and family-centeredness and is willing to consider innovative approaches to achieve these improvements (Zimring, Augenbroe, Malone, & Sadler, 2008). However, it is certainly possible for a well-conceived evidence-based project to test important concepts or hypotheses and still yield poor outcomes. Such is the nature of experimental science. For example, not all research produces the cure for cancer. Scientific research is a laborious process that proposes, tests, and rejects many ideas, combines the results of prior efforts in new ways, and continues to improve the model with each successive piece of information that emerges (Hamilton, 2003).

Ideally, integration of the EBD process should begin after an organization has decided to undertake a construction project and is
in the process of defining its EBD goals and objectives. Research
plays a pivotal role in evidence-based design. It is through research that design solutions are empirically evaluated and scientific evidence is created.

In fact, the very term itself, evidence-based design (EBD) contains
two inseparable elements: evidence and design. Evidence—that
which tends to prove or disprove something (Webster's American
Dictionary, 2000)—is gathered through research. Research data
may already exist in previous studies, may already exist but may
need to be organized (that is, internal data recorded by healthcare
facilities), or may need to be collected in a new research study.
Guide 2: Building the Evidence Base discusses the key elements
of EBD research and the detailed research process of using existing evidence and creating new evidence. Guide 2 also details the
different types, methods, and levels of research and how to more
closely examine, evaluate, and use existing evidence. Finally, it
explains how to conduct research to test design decisions and innovations and add to the knowledge base.

This chapter serves as a primer by providing a brief overview of
how to use research to inform design, understand and evaluate
evidence, and how to create new evidence.

■■ USING RESEARCH TO INFORM DESIGN

Linking research and design is the core of evidence-based design.
In fact, what differentiates EBD from a typical design approach
is its emphasis on using research to support design decisions and
evaluation of design innovations. Individuals practicing evidence-
based design use research throughout the lifecycle of the facility
or project. As the following material demonstrates, EBD plays a
vital role during different stages of the project.

Predesign and Design

Research is vital during predesign and design. After the vision and goals and objectives for the project have been developed, a review of literature can help to evaluate existing design options and spark design innovations. This is also the time during which individuals practicing evidence-based design develop a hypothesis and obtain and translate evidence into design. In addition, individuals practicing evidence-based design might use a small-scale research project to test the effectiveness of a product or design innovation and, thus, help them decide to go forward with a larger scale project.

Research in Practice at PeaceHealth

Stakeholders should use research to understand which environmental elements are the best design options to improve outcomes. For example, Ulrich et al (2008) reference literature to understand the impact of ceiling lifts on staff outcomes: "Many studies have been undertaken to evaluate the physical stress and strain caused by patient handling. *Ceiling lifts* have consistently been identified to reduce the incidence of injury and the cost of injury claims" (pp. 100-101).

PeaceHealth in Eugene, Oregon, has put this into practice in its new Sacred Heart Medical Center (SHMC). Like most health systems, PeaceHealth confronted a significant number of back injuries involved in lifting and moving patients. During the planning stage for SHMC, PeaceHealth explored several mechanical devices in an existing facility by testing them in concert with a no-manual-lift policy.

Based on the evidence available about the benefits of using ceiling lifts, PeaceHealth installed ceiling lifts in 26 of 33 intensive-care unit (ICU) rooms at its River Bend, Oregon facility in late 2002 and in all 24 neurology rooms in late 2003. Incident reports obtained from both

---

units spanned a period of 60 months (January 2001 to December 2006). The ICU had 10 injuries related to patient handling in the two years before installation of ceiling lifts. Annual cost of patient-handling injuries was $142,500.After lifts were installed in more than 75% of the rooms, there were no injuries during the study period caused by moving patients using the lifts (Joseph & Fritz, 2006).

In neurology, there were 15 injuries related to patient handling in the three years before the installation of ceiling lifts. The annual cost of patient handling injuries in this unit was $222,645. In the two years since installation on the unit, there have been six injuries, some with extenuating circumstances (for example, failure to use the lift or a combative patient). The annual cost in neurology after lift installation was $54,660.

Based on the dramatic findings of the study, PeaceHealth made all 309 rooms lift ready and installed 234 transverse rails and lifts in their new facility. They project a return on investment in two-and-a-half years in the new facility.

—Evidence for Innovation: Transforming Children's Health Through the Physical Environment: A collaboration of National Association of Children's Hospitals and Related Institutions and The Center for Health Design, 2008.

Research can also improve communication by providing a common language between stakeholders, help designers to effectively communicate with owners over competing design options and make it easier to resolve possible disagreements. Finally, research can also facilitate the tracking of the design process. By documenting the design process, research can provide information for future review.

Construction and Occupancy

During and after the construction and occupancy phases, research can be used to evaluate the effectiveness of design strategies. Do the selected design strategies work better than alternatives? How do the chosen design strategies influence outcomes? Research can help answer these questions and provide valuable data on the effectiveness of the design strategies, such as sound-absorbing ceiling tiles, daylight, and healing gardens.

The Use of Research after Occupancy: The Children's Hospital

Due to a military base closure, The Children's Hospital, Aurora, Colorado, capitalized on a once-in-a-lifetime opportunity to build a total replacement pediatric hospital on a greenfield site and evaluate the outcomes of a facility designed and built with the best available evidence.

All nursing, social work, therapy, housekeeping staff, and families and selected inpatient units participated in pre- and post-surveys. The hospital collected data in the original facility six months prior to its move and six months post move and will collect again at 12 months post-move. Other data collected at these intervals include nosocomial infection rates, staffing (ratios and turnover), workflow, skill mix, and variance reports. Several initial findings have surfaced, but none more dramatic than the change in staff turnover. Pre-move turnover data from October 2007 reflected a nurse turnover of 9.55% per year. The March 2008 nursing turnover rate, six months post-move was 4.38%. This result shows that the hospital was able to achieve its stated goal of attracting and maintaining staff.

—Evidence for Innovation: Transforming Children's Health Through the Physical Environment: *A collaboration of* National Association of Children's Hospitals and Related Institutions *and The Center for Health Design, 2008.*

Research can also be used to test theories. Findings can be used to test whether the evidence supports the hypotheses derived from certain theories. Based on the results, researchers may refine theories and test them further in a second round of research. Finally, new research contributes to the existing knowledge base. Research findings should be published; good research studies make great contributions to the field and significantly expand the knowledge base.

■■ UNDERSTANDING AND EVALUATING EVIDENCE

Quality research and the application of research findings underpin the entire EBD effort, providing confidence and credibility to value-driven decisions made by leaders. Ulrich and Zimring's sentinel literature review commissioned by The Center for Health Design in 2004 provided a framework that linked hospital design with clinical outcomes. After reviewing thousands of articles, the team identified more than 600 studies, most from peer-reviewed journals, that provide strong evidence confirming that certain design characteristics impact patient and staff outcomes in four key areas:

- reduction in staff stress and fatigue
- improvement in patient safety
- reduction in patient stress
- improvement in overall healthcare quality

Ulrich et al (2008) completed a second analysis of the literature from 2004 to 2007 that included an extensive search for empirical studies linking the design of the physical environments of hospitals with healthcare outcomes. This is an example of collecting information from existing sources. The authors screened all identified references using several criteria. The studies had to be empirically based and peer reviewed. In addition, Ulrich et al evaluated the quality of each study's research design and methods. They found a large number of rigorous studies that established a

According to Stichler (2009), "a peer-reviewed journal is a scholarly publication that requires that each article submitted be critically appraised by an independent panel of subject experts who are peers of the author ... Peer review is the undisputed cornerstone of scientific writing; its purpose is to ensure that the published content—both information and data—is of the highest quality" (p. 70-71).

relationship between hospital design and outcomes. They identified three main categories of outcomes:

- patient safety issues, such as infections, medical errors and falls
- other patient outcomes, such as pain, sleep, stress, and depression, length of stay, spatial orientation, privacy, communication, social support, and overall patient satisfaction
- staff outcomes, such as injuries, stress, work effectiveness, and satisfaction (Ulrich et al, 2008)

Since the 2004 study, Ulrich et al (2008) found that the body of evidence (Table 2) has grown to substantial numbers due to the urgent need for better healthcare facilities. This evidence makes it clear that facilities have the capability to make hospitals "less risky and stressful, promoting more healing for patients, and providing better places for staff to work" (p. 63).

"In medical fields, a randomized controlled trial or experiment is considered the strongest research design for generating sound and credible empirical evidence" (Ulrich et al, 2008, p.63). In the review of EBD literature, the researchers found few of these randomized controlled trials that directly linked design strategies to healthcare outcomes. Because so many environmental features are impacted by physical changes, confounding variables are created, making it difficult to link the impact on the healthcare outcomes to one independent effect.

Specifically, Ulrich et al (2008) stated:

Although many studies may not be well-controlled, the strength of the evidence is enhanced by the fact that, in the case of certain environmental factors, *reliable patterns of findings* across several studies emerged with respect to outcome influences. Furthermore, these patterns were broadly consistent with predictions

Due to a large amount of research findings, Ulrich et al (2008) concluded that "one critically important way that EBD improves safety is by reducing the risk of hospital-acquired infections (that is, nosocomial infections), a leading cause of death in the United States. One general conclusion supported by the infection literature is that the design of the physical environment impacts nosocomial infection rates by affecting all three major transmission routes—air, contact, and water ... There is a pattern across scores of studies indicating that infection rates are lower when there is very good air and water quality and greater physical separation, isolation, or space per patient" (p. 64).

Table 2:
Summary of the Relationship Between Design Factors and Healthcare Outcomes

Healthcare Outcomes \ Design Strategies or Environmental Interventions	Single-bed rooms	Access to daylight	Appropriate lighting	Views of nature	Family zone in patient rooms	Carpeting	Noise-reducing finishes	Ceiling lifts	Nursing floor layout	Decentralized supplies	Acuity-adaptable rooms
Reduce hospital-acquired infections	**										
Reduce medical errors	*		*				*				*
Reduce patient falls	*		*		*	*			*		*
Reduce pain		*	*	**			*				
Improve patients' sleep	**	*	*				*				
Reduce patient stress	*	*	*	**	*		**				
Reduce depression		**	**	*	*						
Reduce length of stay		*	*	*							*
Improve patient privacy and confidentiality	**					*	*				
Improve communication with patients and family members	**					*	*				
Improved social support	*				*	*					
Increase patient satisfaction	**	*	*	*	*	*	*				
Decrease staff injuries									**		*
Decrease staff stress	*	*	*	*			*				
Increase staff effectiveness	*		*				*		*	*	*
Increase staff satisfaction	*	*	*	*			*				

* indicates that a relationship between the specific design factor and healthcare outcome was indicated, directly or indirectly, by empirical studies reviewed in this report.

** indicates that there is especially strong evidence (converging findings from multiple rigorous studies) indicating that a design intervention improves a healthcare outcome.

Source: Reprinted here with permission (Ulrich et al 2008).

based on established knowledge and theory concerning environment and healthcare outcomes … Future research should be carefully designed and controlled so that the independent role of specific environmental changes or interventions can be better understood (p. 63–64).

The following sections discuss the kinds of possible data measurements and from where these data can be accessed. Research will provide stronger evidence about the influence of design if it includes more specific measures of environmental components and an individual's exposure to environmental features over time.

■■ CREATING NEW EVIDENCE

As stated in Chapter Two, healthcare delivery systems can be expressed by the environment of care (EOC), which is comprised of six components:

- delivery of care model (concepts)
- facility and service users (people)
- systems design
- layout and operational planning
- physical environment
- design process and implementation

Measurements of some of the EOC components include the daily changes in temperature, light, sound, location, dimension, distance, materials, furnishings, or equipment used in the care setting. As discussed previously, data may already exist through previous studies, may already exist but need organizing (for example, internal data from surveys, databases), or may need to be created. Every healthcare organization records a great deal of data that indicate the health status of patients—performance, safety, injury, and error rates among staff, costs of care, and care outcomes, along with economic and operational factors that include satisfaction scores and the return on investment of the facility, its staff, and functionality.

Measures regarding health status are routinely collected along with the body of laboratory and diagnostic data recorded on all patients during the course of their care. Such information is stored in healthcare charts and databases according to carefully prescribed protocols and best-practice guidelines that have been validated over many years of research and clinical use, with very large samples. Given institutional approval, this database of information can be mined to explore how changes to the built environment relate to health, performance, satisfaction, and economic outcomes.

If individuals practicing evidence-based design need to gather data that does not yet exist, they should carefully assess the measurement devices to ensure that the environmental variable being studied is valid and reliable. For example, recent circadian research suggests that short wavelength light (Brainard et al, 2001) is particularly effective in suppressing melatonin-induced sleepiness (Figueiro et al, 2006) and that long-wavelength red light influences cardiac reactivity (Edelstein et al, 2006). However, typical photometers have the greatest accuracy in the green range of light and are relatively inaccurate when measuring short-wavelength blue light and long-wavelength red light. In a similar manner, dosimeters are filtered to measure sound intensities in the central range of speech frequencies, but they are less accurate at measuring high and low frequencies and rapid impact sounds.

With the selection of more sophisticated measurement devices, a broader range of information about environmental factors can be collected and correlated with the wealth of health and performance information currently recorded at all healthcare institutions (Edelstein et al, 2006).

Survey data are also routinely collected by healthcare providers (for example, Arbor, Press Ganey, the Hospital Consumer Assessment of Healthcare Providers and Systems [HCAHPS], etc.) to reveal patient comments and satisfaction with their healthcare experience. While these surveys ask general questions about the environment of care, they do not ask about environmental features with enough specificity to determine which factors of the built environment influenced their answers or how design influences their exposure to features of the built environment. Therefore, a specific causal relationship between design and patient satisfaction cannot be directly asserted.

For example, the HCAHPS survey asks patients about communication with the medical team. A low score on this topic could arise because the medical team had poor communication skills despite spending a long time with the patient or because the team spent little time communicating with the patient. Alternatively, the team may have excellent communication skills and contact time but could not be heard by the patient due to surrounding noise levels or the patient's inability to hear speech clearly, lip-read, or watch facial expressions (such as communication in dark imaging rooms).

Indeed, a better design of the patient environment might provide spaces to support difficult communication, decrease the time spent at bedside, or increase a patient's ability to hear or comprehend speech in the presence of unwanted noise. However, without specific measures of the built conditions surrounding the behavior reported, it is difficult to assert that design hypotheses were supported or that design strategies were effective in improving outcomes, and thus researchers can only make suppositions about the relationship between design change and outcome measures.

In summary, to assert causal relationships between features of the built environment and outcomes, equally specific information about the built environment must be recorded over time and be relative to patient and staff exposure during their time within that setting. Once these causal relationships have been properly measured, the evidence should be translated into application. Design solutions based on the original hypotheses along with supporting literature may then be developed and mocked-up or built and studied.

Research builds the scientific knowledge base that healthcare administrators, planners, and designers can use to make decisions. Thus, a basic knowledge of EBD research is important so that individuals practicing evidence-based design can use research to inform, understand and evaluate evidence, and create new evidence by participating in research activities. Refer to *Guide 2: Building the Evidence Base* for more information.

CHAPTER THREE REVIEW QUESTIONS

1. How is *research* defined in the context of evidence-based design?
2. How can existing data within a healthcare facility be used in EBD, given institutional approval?
3. Strong evidence has confirmed that certain design characteristics impact patient and staff outcomes in four key areas. What are these key areas?
4. What are three sources for relevant data that could be found within the healthcare organization itself?
5. In what ways can the research process improve communication among team members?

NOTES

_____

_____

_____

_____

_____

_____

_____

_____

_____

To check your answers see Appendix C

CHAPTER THREE QUIZ QUESTIONS

1. The EBD process is differentiated from the typical design process because it _____.

    a. involves staff in design decision making

    b. uses research to develop and evaluate design innovations

    c. changes the composition of the interdisciplinary design team

2. Ideally, EBD research can be used during and after the construction and occupancy phases to _____.

    a. develop hypotheses about how the design decisions may impact outcomes

    b. evaluate the effectiveness of design solutions

    c. alter parts of the design as it becomes clear whether or not decisions were appropriate

3. At which phase of the project should stakeholders use research to understand which environmental elements are the best design options to improve outcomes?

    a. predesign/design

    b. construction

    c. occupancy

4. Specific information about the built environment recorded over time and relative to patient and staff exposure during their time within that setting is needed to assert _____ relationships between features of the built environment and outcomes.

    a. theoretical

    b. correlational

    c. causal

List the key steps of an EBD process.

 Provide examples of several healthcare organizations that have implemented or started the EBD journey.

Chapter Four at a Glance

The Evidence-Based Design Process in Application

■∎ INTRODUCTION

Chapter 1 explores the history and evolution of EBD up to its present definition, which according to The Center for Health Design (2008b), is the process of basing decisions about the built environment on credible research to achieve the best possible outcomes. The chapter also defines the key steps for an EBD process, which include:

- Define evidence-based goals and objectives.
- Find sources for relevant evidence.
- Critically interpret relevant evidence.
- Create and innovate evidence-based design concepts.
- Develop a hypothesis.
- Collect baseline performance measures.
- Monitor implementation of design and construction.
- Measure post-occupancy performance results.

Chapter 1 also reviews the trends and challenges facing the healthcare delivery system.

Chapter 2 goes on to define the various healthcare settings and the critical role that stakeholders and leadership play in the EBD process. The chapter also touches on the impact of the Environment of Care components to be considered during design and their impact on healthcare organizational culture during the EBD process.

Finally, Chapter 3 provides a high-level introduction of the important role of research and the use of evidence in EBD, as well as the importance of creating new evidence. In addition, the chapter offers an overview of the most current evidence as identified by Ulrich et al (2008) followed by a brief discussion about the credibility of the evidence.

Over the years, a number of approaches to the EBD process have been implemented, as pioneering organizations have taken the nascent knowledge and adapted it to their unique set of circumstances. In spite of the different circumstances, one thing is certain: EBD is a process that can be integrated into any stage of the building design process, although it is optimized when implemented from the beginning of the project.

Incorporating the key EBD steps in practice requires commitment and the careful coordination between healthcare organizations, design and construction firms, and research expertise. This chapter provides examples of how several healthcare organizations and systems have implemented or started the EBD journey. These illustrate real-life applications and interpretations of the EBD process. As these examples illustrate, each healthcare system executes the key EBD steps in its own way; however, the key steps *are* addressed. Individuals that practice evidence-based design apply evidence in design and conduct research so that results add to the growing body of evidence. Members of the interdisciplinary team have the opportunity to produce better outcomes for patients, families, staff, and the environment.

Showcased in the following materials are examples of the EBD process as conducted by various healthcare organizations; examples include some of The Center for Health Design's Pebble Projects. In addition, the Military Health System's (MHS) framework, which includes a series of EBD checklists, is shared for consideration. The MHS is in the process of applying EBD across the life cycle for all their medical facilities. MHS leaders are committed to sharing their tools and experiences gained during this on-going journey in order to improve the outcomes for patients and families, the staff who care for them, and to contribute to the growing body of evidence (Ossmann, Dellinger and Boenecke, 2008).

■■ PEBBLE PROJECT EXAMPLES

Blending the Old and New: Bronson Methodist Hospital

Bronson Methodist Hospital opened its doors in Kalamazoo, Michigan, in December 2000 with a $210 million replacement facility. The project was designed to be a unique healing environment using art, music, nature, and light. The facility has become recognized as a best practice site for hospital facility design and has garnered significant national attention.

Well-known for high-quality care and its all-private room facility, Bronson has experienced a more than 40% increase in patients since the facility opened (as noted in Chapter 1). Based on this increase, Bronson decided to expand patient-care services to a location on its former campus, adjacent to the new hospital. It was determined that renovating the existing inpatient tower (North Pavilion) would result in significant time and cost savings, and suit the hospital's master plan for long-term growth.

The architecture and engineering firm, Diekema Hamann, was challenged to keep Bronson's "new hospital" reputation and patient experience alive within the confines of an existing structure. From a broad view, the firm overcame this challenge by ensuring that the North

Pavilion included the following EBD solutions:

- Natural lighting, landscape views, and indoor gardens and courtyards to reduce patient stress
- Open welcoming public spaces, corridors, and waiting areas
- Enhanced sound reduction through the use of special glazing, high-performance acoustic ceilings, and floor selections
- Simplified wayfinding
- Home-like, adaptable labor and delivery rooms that increase safety, decrease patient transfers, and minimize noise and disruption
- A neonatal intensive care unit that provides all-private rooms—a pioneering design concept

Like Bronson's new hospital, the North Pavilion is the cumulative result of wide-ranging EBD solutions. By blending old with new, this revitalized facility achieves the extraordinary for patients and staff.

—*"Blending Old and New to Achieve the Extraordinary,"* Healthcare Design Magazine, *April, 2008.*

PeaceHealth goes Lean

PeaceHealth moved its main hospital, Sacred Heart Medical Center (SHMC), to a property called RiverBend in Springfield, Oregon. With its spectacular location on the McKenzie River and proximity to Interstate 5, it is accessible to both local metro cities and the entire SHMC regional service area. SHMC provides the necessary space to build for current needs with expansion space for the future. The goals were to build a state-of-the-art medical center in a unique natural setting that is a healing environment for patients, staff, and visitors, create a facility that supports patient- and family-centered care that is flexible, expandable, and adaptable.

Its Pebble Project will measure the impact of the above goals. The project actively uses Lean principles to guide design and measure outcomes. In addition, the principles of renewable and sustainable design, stewardship of the environment, responsible land use and transportation planning, and the incorporation of public amenities and open spaces guided development at RiverBend. The design and construction phases of the project were completed in 2008. The project architect is Anshen+Allen Architects.

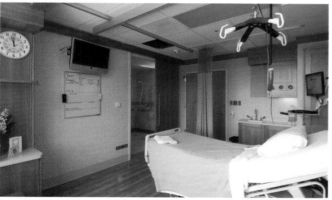

Source: Reprinted with permission. Sacred Heart Medical Center at Riverbend, 2010.

According to the Institute for Healthcare Improvement (IHI), "Lean thinking begins with driving out waste so that all work adds value and serves the customer's needs. Identifying value-added and non-value-added steps in every process is the beginning of the journey toward lean operations.

In order for lean principles to take root, leaders must first work to create an organizational culture that is receptive to lean thinking. The commitment to lean must start at the very top of the organization, and all staff should be involved in helping to redesign processes to improve flow and reduce waste" (2005, abstract).

Dublin Methodist Hospital

Dublin Methodist Hospital in Dublin, Ohio, opened its doors in January 2008. To date, no other hospital has been constructed that implements so comprehensively what is known about the connection between design of the built environment and the outcomes it can affect.

Source: Reprinted with permission. CAMA, Inc. (Designer), Karlsberger (Architect), Feinknopf Photography.

The project team and hospital leadership shared a common belief that EBD strategies can improve the emotional and physical well-being of users as much as it can improve the operational efficiency, the quality of care, and productivity. This belief has been put to the test. Throughout the project, the design team applied out-of-the-box thinking and took measured risks based on existing evidence. Firmly committed to EBD, the team applied research in a sensitive and thoughtful manner that considered elements of healing environments and every user's individual experience.

Research data was incorporated into the project's development and helped create the key guiding principles for the design of the new facility. Throughout the project, the team applied current best practices based on evidence. Examples of the implemented best practices were: large single-patient rooms with ample space to reduce infections, reduce noise, increase privacy, and support family presence in giving care.

Dublin Methodist: Handwashing Sink
The location, quantity, and design of the handwashing sinks were designed to improve compliance and reduce infections. Patient rooms have a strip design built into the floor and up the wall leading to the sink to draw the eye to it—a subliminal cue for staff to wash their hands. Natural daylight and sunlight can be found within the facility to reduce depression, length of stay, and the amount of pain medication administered.

Now that Dublin has been completed and is open and running, the next step will be to collect and analyze the data from the innovations.

—*Dublin Methodist Hospital: Evidence-Based Design at Work,* Healthcare Design Magazine, *February 2008.*

■I THE MILITARY HEALTH SYSTEM

The Military Health System (MHS) identified principles, goals and desired outcomes to guide its application of EBD. "Within the MHS ... there was a strong sense that a convergence of patient centered planning and design processes based on research could positively influence health outcomes, patient safety, and long-term operating efficiencies. These concepts were articulated by a multidisciplinary team...who converged to promote, codify, and implement patient-centered and evidenced-based design throughout the MHS capital facility landscape ... The goals seek to promote the integrity of the clinical encounter, empower the patient, relieve suffering, and promote long-term health and wellness" (Casscells, Kurmel, Ponatoski, 2009, p. 137).

"It is a challenging endeavor to develop and implement system-wide EBD design strategies. The MHS has addressed this challenge by means of policy directives [as directed by former Assistant Secretary of Defense for Health Affairs, William Winkenwerder, MD] and through a framework of 'guiding principles' to implement EBD for all new capital projects" (Casscells, Kurmel, Ponatoski, 2009, p. 137). The following list of principles, corresponding goals, and desired outcomes have been embraced by the MHS "that will influence design decisions for all future military healthcare construction projects" (p. 137):

1. Create a patient and family centered environment reflecting the MHS culture of caring.
   - Increase social support.
   - Reduce spatial disorientation.
   - Improve patient privacy and confidentiality.
   - Provide adequate and appropriate light exposure.
   - Support optimal patient nutrition.

In addition, EBD activities were identified for each phase of the Facility Life Cycle Management and Performance model shown in Figure 6 (Malone, Mann-Dooks, & Strauss, 2007). This model was first conceptualized by the US Army Health Facility Planning Agency in 1996. Most of the following facility lifecycle phases are well-known:

- strategic and business planning, which results in a facility's master plan or portfolio
- project planning, programming, design, construction, commissioning

- ongoing facility operation activities
- building retirement

Transition planning represents an additional phase and ensures that all of the necessary steps are planned and implemented to successfully move the organization from its present state to the envisioned future. Although drawn in a linear fashion, the model does not capture the overlapping of phases—primarily programming, planning, design, and construction phases—to shorten the acquisition time.

The goal is to apply EBD across the full range of Military Health System's facility projects to include replacement hospitals and facilities, major facility additions and renovation work, required life and safety upgrade activities, and, critically, during the routine operational and maintenance activities. EBD activities exist in every phase of the Facility Life Cycle Management and Performance Model, not just the design phase.

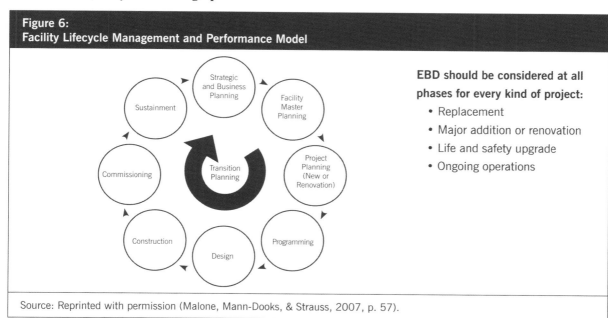

Figure 6:
Facility Lifecycle Management and Performance Model

EBD should be considered at all phases for every kind of project:
- Replacement
- Major addition or renovation
- Life and safety upgrade
- Ongoing operations

Source: Reprinted with permission (Malone, Mann-Dooks, & Strauss, 2007, p. 57).

Military Health System EBD Checklists

In the following sections, each phase of the model will be explained and has an accompanying EBD activity checklist that can be found in Appendix A. The original checklists were first developed for use by the Military Health System to guide a $5 billion portfolio investment projected over the next few years and are contained in a public source document (Malone, Mann-Dooks, & Strauss, 2007). The various EBD activities during each phase foster communication and clarity of purpose between the interdisciplinary team members on the project. These checklists reflect the MHS' ongoing EBD experience.

Strategic Planning

Most healthcare facilities enjoy a 30- to 50-year lifespan, an end point impossible to envision given the constant and rapid evolution of population demand, healthcare-delivery advances, and perennial technology discoveries and improvements. Nevertheless, strategic planning must represent the longest view the leadership team can fathom, which is often only 5 to 10 years. This routine, leader-driven activity provides the framework for all major investment decisions to include facility investments. As stated in Chapter 2, the chief executive officer (CEO) and board of trustees bear special responsibilities with regard to facility strategic planning to fully maximize facility features and capabilities to reach quality and resource goals, in addition to replacing aging infrastructure.

Strategic planning almost always requires a refinement of the organization's vision and mission statements. Successful organizations ensure that all of the key stakeholders are engaged in this critical activity and include patient and family representatives and community leaders. CEOs must clearly state the targeted outcomes they hope to achieve, explaining the targets in measurable outcomes—including financial measures—that will be more fully discussed in the business planning phases. Further, CEOs can share compelling stories to ensure that all of the team members understand what is at stake. (See Appendix A for the detailed strategic EBD questions and activities checklist.)

Business Planning

All investments require a value proposition evaluation and a business plan, whether the investment represents new equipment, adding services, or growing existing service lines or facility capital investments. The value proposition provides a clear, concise description of the tangible outcomes expected as a result of one investment choice over another to include any of the design strategies. Business planning translates the current and strategic state in terms of costs and revenues with regard to these investments.

Many design strategies require front-end investment and may incur more operational costs than a more traditional approach over the facility's life. Historically, facility infrastructure has been viewed as a sunk cost or a continuing overhead cost, frequently described as the cost per square foot of the facility, both to build and maintain. What is missing completely is an understanding of how the building itself contributes to the heart of the healthcare business: improving patient, family, and staff outcomes and the cost avoidance or revenue enhancement associated with each. (See Appendix A for the detailed business planning EBD questions and activities checklist.)

Six Key Investment Questions

Sadler et al (2008) identified six key questions for hospital leaders to consider when contemplating a major building project:

- Urgency: Is the project needed now to fulfill the hospital's mission?

- Appropriateness: Is the proposed plan the most reasonable and prudent choice in light of other alternatives?
- Cost: Is the cost per square foot appropriate in light of other projects being built in the region?
- Financial impact: Has the financial impact of additional volume, depreciation expense, and revenue assumptions been reasonably analyzed and projected?
- Source of funds: Is the anticipated combination of additional operating income, reserves, borrowing, and philanthropy reasonable and enough to support the project?
- Evidence-based design features: Will the proposed project incorporate all the relevant and proven EBD innovations to optimize patient safety, quality, and satisfaction, as well as work-force safety, satisfaction, productivity, and energy efficiency?

Return-on-investment Framework for Evaluating Design Strategies

A return-on-investment (ROI) is a common tool used by chief financial officers to financially evaluate major investment decisions in terms of cost and revenue. Each design strategy has an associated cost and a potential ROI. For the most part, the market only considers the initial EBD front-end investment cost for a facility project, with little consideration given to the impact on design strategy costs associated with operations, maintenance, and repair over the facility's life. Most importantly, little work has been done to link design strategies with specific improvements in patient, family, and staff outcomes expressed in financial terms.

Each organization will need to incorporate the latest evidence and best judgment about cost and revenue impacts of design innovations. Almost everything can be financially quantified.

For example, if the goal is to reduce hospital-associated infections (HAIs), use the following steps:

1. Identify the planned design strategies as part of an integrated bundle of solutions, such as 100% single-patient rooms, a visible and easily accessible staff sink in each room, increased number of alcohol gel disinfection devices, and increased HEPA filtration in those areas where highly vulnerable patients receive care.
2. Estimate the associated initial and life cycle investment costs for each design strategy. This step represents the cost side of the ROI equation.
3. Identify the revenue returns by quantifying the financial impact of HAIs, comparing the costs for patients who did and did not develop a HAI. (Some revenue improvements due to fewer HAIs might also include reduced litigation and settlement costs, improved bond rating, and avoidance of non-reimbursements). The difference in costs between the two groups of patients represents the cost-avoidance opportunity.
4. Identify by number or percent the reduced number of HAI cases which becomes the cost avoidance target. The second part of the revenue side of the equation is an estimate of the additional number of patients who could be cared for because there would be fewer patients who develop a HAI due to longer hospitalizations. These two variables represent the enhanced revenue opportunity.
5. Subtracting the costs from the enhanced revenue over time provides the ROI analysis for CEOs, CFOs, and the board of trustees to demonstrate the impact of EBD investments on the bottom line.

A detailed ROI framework methodology is provided in *Study Guide 3: Integrating Evidence-Based Design.*

Facility Master Planning

A number of large healthcare organizations own and operate more than just a single building at any single location to provide patient-care services. The facility portfolio master plan provides an overview of the facility capital resources for a healthcare organization and includes:

- an inventory of all healthcare facilities
- a facility condition assessment of each building
- a functional assessment of the current space, including the missing but desired design strategies
- a statement of future workload demand and its effect on space needs
- a concept of operations for the missions supported in each of the buildings
- a description of future capital investments specific to mission, scope, cost, and schedule, including those with new design strategies

(See Appendix A for the detailed facility master planning EBD questions and activities checklist.)

Transition Planning

Transition planning begins the moment a decision is made to pursue a capital investment project and includes all of the activities needed to move the organization literally and figuratively from the current to the future state. This comprehensive step-by-step process identifies all of the changes required to achieve the desired outcome, which can include changes to policies and procedures, necessary staff orientation, training and equipment familiarization, a communications plan, and a patient move plan, just to name a few. The success of transition planning is frequently measured during the post-occupancy evaluation process. (See Appendix A for the detailed transition planning EBD questions and activities checklist.)

Project Planning

Once a project is approved, the details must be specified for each clinical or administrative area included in the project:

- vision/mission statement (scope of services, training, and research)
- work volumes (historic compared with future)
- staffing (historic compared with future)
- key operating assumptions and parameters
- desired adjacencies
- desired layout and workflow
- major equipment
- design strategies

Good project planning involves key interdisciplinary stakeholders who best understand current operations for each hospital area and can envision the future with regard to their discipline. Specialty consultants are frequently engaged to assist in the identification of future care, equipment, and technology trends. Project planning also considers the project schedule, which is particularly important in retrofit projects that require moving services to a temporary location to accomplish the work. Understanding the desired EBD outcomes and articulating the vision remains key to design success. (See Appendix A for the detailed project planning EBD questions and activities checklist.)

Programming

The American Institute of Architects' (AIA) 2006 *Guidelines for Design and Construction of Health Care Facilities* is the reference most used by healthcare planners, architects, and engineers involved in planning for healthcare renovation and construction (AIA, 2006). (The 2010 Edition of the *Guidelines for Design and Construction of Health Care Facilities* was released in January 2010). Programmers use the guidelines and other support material such

Visioning sessions with key patient, staff, and community members are often a helpful means to launch the project and clarify the project message, image, brand, or theme, as well as identify desired features or amenities and services to be included in the project. As the design concludes, these signature elements can then be translated into a project experience map, which reflects both the interior and wayfinding design that can be used in a meaningful way by patients, their families, and the healthcare team.

as EBD research to determine the number and size of required rooms to support the described concept of operation for each area in the healthcare organization. Many design strategies require no additional programmed space. (See Appendix A for the detailed programming EBD questions and activities checklist.)

Design

Design involves the creation of blueprints used by builders to construct the building. Many different blueprints are produced by the various disciplines, to include: schematic drawings, furniture, equipment, signage, communications, lighting, HVAC, etc; design strategies can be found in all of them. Designs are submitted in an iterative fashion, from predesign and design to construction and occupancy, based on the design schedule. Often, a third party is asked to conduct an evaluation, called value engineering, during the design process. It is important that the evaluation consider the impact of design strategies on the patient and staff outcomes produced by the facility.

There will be many variables to track throughout the design process, including design strategies. The Military Health System's EBD Design Review Checklist (found in Appendix B) is an important communication tool that summarizes the design strategies and can be used during the design development phase to ensure that the design reflects the overarching EBD principles and goals, by reminding the team of the desired strategies. Failure Modes and Effects Analysis (FMEA) serves as a safety evaluation tool when reviewing emerging project design documents. It was first created in the engineering community to "define, identify, prioritize, and eliminate known or potential failures, problems, errors from the system, design, process of services before they reach a customer" (Reiling, 2007, p. 37). Teams should consider healthcare facility historic sentinel events or high-volume untoward occurrences and evaluate each

The US General Services Administration defines value engineering "as an organized effort directed at analyzing designed building features, systems, equipment, and material selections for the purpose of achieving essential functions at the lowest lifecycle cost consistent with required performance, quality, reliability, and safety" (US General Services Administration, 2008).

in the context of the design. (See Appendix A for the detailed design EBD questions and activities checklist.)

Construction

The construction phase is when the facility is built and includes the placement of equipment and casework integral to the building. In the past, construction followed the design phase, but concerted efforts are under way to shorten the time between the decision to begin a project and facility occupancy. Today, the construction of many projects begins before design is finalized. The construction phase makes the project real for everyone and is also when the most intense transition planning activities occur, especially those that relate to the transformation of the culture and clinical and administrative process re-engineering. The groundbreaking ceremony provides an opportunity to highlight the planned design strategies meant to improve patient, staff, and resource outcomes.

Many materials are used during the course of construction. Evidence-based design strives to exclude those materials that are proven harmful to the comfort and health of installers and occupants. (See Appendix A for the detailed construction EBD questions and activities checklist.)

Commissioning and Occupancy

Commissioning the facility is the phase when the building is outfitted with everything needed to make it ready for patient care services: furniture, remaining equipment, artwork, and all the additional materials needed to care for patients. Equipment will be certified during commissioning with the appropriate federal or state regulatory agencies. Occupancy occurs when patients are moved from the existing facility to the new space. This can occur in one day, be phased in over many days, or take place when the doors are opened for a new hospital. Occupancy represents the first few days of a facility's long life. (See Appendix A for the detailed commissioning and occupancy EBD questions and activities checklist.)

Operations

The operations phase begins when the building is occupied; it represents the longest phase of a facility's life. Post-occupancy EBD evaluations should be conducted to include the post-occupancy measures associated with the targeted improvement goals for which design strategies were invested. Comparing and sharing the pre- and post-occupancy measures is a critical activity that contributes to the field's growing understanding of how the physical environment contributes to patient and staff outcomes and the bottom line. Completing and publishing the results of these comparisons and lessons learned is an important step for broadening the EBD field. Routine maintenance and repair activities and expected renovations, over time, provide additional opportunities to inject design strategies. (See Appendix A for the detailed operations EBD questions and activities checklist.)

■I SUMMARY OF EVIDENCE-BASED DESIGN

In summary, evidence-based design entails a deliberate planning, implementation, and evaluation approach that can be managed in bite-sized efforts for all projects. It is most important to first establish EBD goals and objectives that will inform and guide the project, which together with other interventions, result in outcomes one hopes to achieve. The EBD process can be implemented in multiple ways, as made clear by the examples presented in this chapter. However, each healthcare organization must develop a process that reflects the strategic vision and goals of their organization and incorporate the key EBD steps outlined in this chapter. *Guide 3 Integrating Evidence-Based Design* further elaborates on the integration of the EBD steps within an entire project.

The timing for EBD could not be more critical considering the healthcare construction boom already underway that is providing the unique opportunity to demonstrate how the largest capital investment for a healthcare organization—the building—can be used as a tool to improve desired patient, staff, environmental, and resource outcomes. More EBD research is needed and should be applied as a component of a bundle of solutions: reengineered clinical and business processes; a transformed organizational culture; and focused leadership committed to disciplined implementation and evaluation. Clearly this is complex work, but it is achievable when broken down into activities across the facility's life cycle, as illustrated by pioneers described throughout this guide.

The stakes are high for the most personal service provided—healthcare. Every healthcare stakeholder—families, friends, and communities—will be impacted by the successes and failures of design. Looking forward, EBD means new and higher expectations from everyone regarding design that makes a difference in the lives of patients, families, and staff. Envision a world where all healthcare environments are created using an EBD process, resulting in improvements in patient-care quality, safety and satisfaction, staff safety and job satisfaction, and in environmental safety, all while improving healthcare organizational goals. Evidence-based design is an important tool to change healthcare for the better.

As Sir Winston Churchill remarked,
"We shape our buildings and afterwards our buildings shape us."
-May 10, 1941

CHAPTER FOUR REVIEW QUESTIONS

1. List the key steps in an EBD process.
2. What is the value of conducting visioning sessions with key patient, staff, and community members when launching the project?

NOTES

_____

_____

_____

_____

_____

_____

_____

_____

_____

_____

_____

To check your answers see Appendix C

CHAPTER FOUR QUIZ QUESTIONS

1. The EBD process can be integrated into _____ stage of the building design process.

    a. the predesign/design

    b. the construction

    c. any

2. The phase when the building is outfitted with everything needed to make it ready for patient care services is called the _____.

    a. programming phase

    b. commissioning phase

    c. occupancy phase

■▌APPENDIX A: THE MILITARY HEALTH SYSTEM'S EVIDENCE-BASED DESIGN CHECKLISTS

The Military Health System originally developed the following checklists to guide a $5 billion portfolio investment projected over the next few years. Subsequently, the checklists have been refined to reflect MHS's ongoing evidence-based design (EBD) experience.

Strategic EBD Questions/Activities Checklist

Identifying Problems Requiring Resolution and Potential EBD Solutions

What problems are you trying to solve for which the facility infrastructure and EBD may play an important role? Please remember to illuminate the answers with real examples and stories from your facility. Some target outcome goals are suggested below:

- Improving patient safety and hospital reimbursement by reducing hospital-acquired infections, patient falls and injuries, and medication errors. What are your current rates for each?
- Improving additional hospital-acquired conditions for which the Centers for Medicare and Medicaid Services or your state may no longer provide reimbursement and EBD may play a role (for example, deep-vein thrombosis and pressure ulcers).
- Improving patient and family-member satisfaction with care. Do you currently measure satisfaction with regard to patients and family, social support, privacy, and confidentiality, sleep and rest, access to healthy food, communication and education, spatial orientation, exposure to natural light, and positive distractions? If so, what are your current rates?
- Improving direct patient-care costs as a result of shorter hospitalizations, decreased use of medications, and more. What is your current bed capacity, occupancy rate, and inpatient bed demand? What is your cost per admission or cost per human life covered?
- Reducing staff injuries associated with patient handling, such as back and other musculoskeletal injuries, workplace violence, and needle-stick injuries. What are your current staff injury

rates for each, and what is the associated financial impact (for example, employee compensation, sick-time salary, and more expensive contract staff replacement costs)?

- Improving staff performance by reducing staff fatigue, noisy and chaotic environments, improving speech intelligibility, resulting in improved team effectiveness and increased time with patients and families. What are your current staffing ratios and number of adverse patient events?

- Improving staff satisfaction and retention rates by reducing the work burden and improving the workplace conditions, thereby reducing staff turnover and consequent staff recruitment, orientation, and training investment requirements. What are your current rates and subsequent financial impact?

- Increasing market share and philanthropy because of improved patient- and family-care outcomes, as well as communitywide and staff satisfaction. What specific growth are you targeting by demographic and services? What is the current level of philanthropic donations?

Prioritize Targets

What EBD solutions exist for the identified problems?

- Prioritize the problems requiring resolution.

Understanding and Leading the Commitment to Change

Do the vision and mission statements reflect the desired future state?

Will a patient-focused–care philosophy drive the effort and decisions made? How will patients, family members, and community representatives be included in this effort?

For each prioritized problem requiring resolution, what clinical and business processes require re-engineering?

Cultural transformation, led from the top, underpins every successful EBD experience. Are all of the key stakeholders engaged? Each problem requiring resolution may need a unique team.

Measuring Success
What metrics are used today to measure the problems requiring resolution?

Are the metrics adequate to measure success at a national level? Use national measures (for example, CDC's National Health and Safety Network methods) whenever possible to improve the generalizability of the findings. Locally derived measures have significant limitations for use outside of the studied facility.

What additional metrics are needed for preoccupancy measurement to occur? Pay particular attention to the financial measure using a lifecycle approach. See the Business Planning section below.

What are the patient, staff, and resource outcome targets that will be realized as a consequence of a comprehensive EBD approach?

Business Planning EBD Questions/Activities Checklist
Have the six key investment questions been answered: urgency, appropriateness, cost, financial impact, source of funds, and EBD features?

Has a return on investment analysis for desired EBD features been completed to include:

- all initial and lifecycle costs
- projected revenue enhancement because of projected improvements in patient and staff outcomes

Facility Master Planning EBD Questions/Activities Checklist

What EBD features are lacking in existing healthcare facilities that might serve as tools to achieve the strategic goals identified? Inventory current facilities, complete an EBD assessment, and refine the EBD return on investment as needed.

What EBD features are planned for future capital investment projects?

Transition Planning EBD Questions/Activities Checklist

What is the transformational theme and leadership approach that frames the communications plan?

- Has a communication plan been developed?
- How will staff members be kept informed about the project and expectations about their roles?
- Are new employees provided with an overview of the project and expectations about their roles?
- How will you engage and communicate with patients and their family members?
- How will key community leaders and partners be engaged and informed?

What EBD features need to be highlighted in transition planning because they represent a significant change in the way care is provided today?

Who are the key stakeholders to involve in EBD feature transition planning?

Are specific resources needed to facilitate EBD future transition planning (for example, mockup or virtual rooms)?

Project Planning EBD Questions/Activities Checklist
Is a visioning session needed to launch the project?

What EBD features are included in the project concept of operations, and what is the EBD research that supports their inclusion?

How will the EBD features be evaluated with regard to impacts on the outcomes described earlier?

How do the EBD features impact all aspects of the concepts of operation?

What clinical or business re-engineering efforts are needed to maximize the facility EBD features?

Is an experience map needed?

Programming EBD Questions/Activities Checklist
Identify specific adjustments in the program to reflect EBD features, so that the total additional amount of space needed to support EBD features can be easily quantified.

Identify specific EBD equipment features such as additional sinks, alcohol-gel disinfectant devices, increased number of HVAC systems that are HEPA-capable, so that these additions can be quantified.

Military Health System's EBD Design Review Checklist
At what point in the design schedule would you expect to find each of the desired EBD features in the blueprints?

Using the Military Health System's EBD Design Review Checklist

(See Appendix B), ensure that all of the EBD features have been captured at each stage of design development.

Does the design support the desired EBD future concepts from all perspectives: patient, family, and visitors, the community, staff, material movement, equipment use, seamless integration with technology, and the digital infrastructure?

Has Failure Modes and Effects Analysis (FMEA) been conducted to ensure that the design does not contribute to risks and failure?

Construction EBD Questions/Activities Checklist

Have the final pre-move outcome measures been captured for those variables expected to be impacted by EBD features?

Has a groundbreaking ceremony been planned that celebrates the EBD features and anticipated impact on patients and their families, as well as the staff and community?

Are the materials *Green Guide for Health Care*-approved and has a checklist been developed to ensure their inclusion?

Are the materials supportive of the desired EBD features?

Is a tree-topping ceremony planned during which EBD green features can be highlighted?

Have precautions been taken to minimize the impact (noise, particles, etc) of construction on adjacent or nearby facilities and their occupants?

Commissioning and Occupancy EBD Questions/Activities Checklist

Have all of the EBD-required furnishings, equipment, and

materials been accounted for? Many checklists are needed to track the myriad items and activities.

What are the planned opening day celebrations? Does the communications plan include press releases and marketing information that highlight the EBD features and expected outcomes of improvements?

Has the post-occupancy evaluation tool to evaluate EBD features been created and tested?

Operations EBD Questions/Activities Checklist

Have the post-occupancy evaluations of EBD features on patient, staff, and resource outcomes been completed at the appropriate times (for example, at 6, 12, and/or 24 months)?

Have the lessons learned been documented and shared broadly? Are there opportunities to insert EBD features with routine maintenance and repair activities, such as:

- high-performance sound-absorbing ceiling tiles
- rubber and carpeted floors where appropriate
- glass that reduces glare
- furnishing replacement and reconfiguration for waiting areas/lounges to provide a residential look
- selection of materials (wall coverings, furniture, etc) with cleanability and low emissions as key considerations
- improved signage
- housekeeping practices that include frequent cleaning of high-contact surfaces
- well-maintained and well-operated ventilation and water supply systems
- green cleaning materials

EBD PRINCIPLE 1: Create a patient- and family-centered environment

	EBD Repsonses and Features	Present	Comment
Increase social support	1. Family zone in patient room. 2. Family respite. 3. Waiting rooms and lounges with comfortable and moveable furniture arranged in small, flexible groupings. 4. Provide a variety of seating to accommodate the widest range of persons. 5. Strive for a residential, not institutional look.		
Reduce spatial disorientation	1. Carefully consider external building cues. 2. Provide visible and easily understood signage (for example, theme approach). 3. Use common language in signs with logical room numbering. 4. Provide directional signs before or at any major intersection. 5. Provide here-you-are maps oriented with the top signifying the direction of movement.		
Provide adequate and appropriate light exposure	1. Provide large windows for access to natural daylight in patient rooms, along with provisions for controlling glare and temperature. 2. Maximize use of natural light. 3. Orient patient rooms to maximize early-morning sun exposure and natural light. 4. Provide high lighting levels for complex visual tasks. 5. Provide windows in staff break rooms when possible.		
Support optimal patient nutrition	1. Provide a design that encourages family participation in patient nutrition. 2. Provide convenient food facilities.		

EBD PRINCIPLE 1: Create a patient- and family-centered environment (continued)

	EBD Repsonses and Features	Present	Comment
Improve patient sleep and rest	1. Single-patient rooms. 2. Noise control. (See EBD principle #2 for features to reduce noise stress.) 3. Comfortable beds and bedding. 4. Maximize exposure to daylight.		
Increase patient privacy and confidentiality	1. Single-patient rooms. 2. Rooms enclosed with walls in areas where patients would be expected to disclose confidential information. 3. Use high-performance sound-absorbing ceiling tiles. 4. Avoid physical proximity between staff and visitors.		
Decrease exposure to harmful chemicals	1. Use 100 percent lead- and cadmium-free roofing, wiring, and paint. 2. Install low-mercury florescent lamps. 3. Use low-emitting VOC and PVC materials. 4. Use materials with no PBDE or phthalates. 5. Minimize use of furniture and furnishings that contain no more than one: PBDE, PFA, urea-formaldehyde, phthalate, and plasticizers		

EBD PRINCIPLE 2: Improve the quality and safety of healthcare delivery

	EBD Repsonses and Features	Present	Comment
Reduce airborne-transmitted infections	1. Single-patient rooms. 2. Maximize HEPA (99.97 percent) filtration for appropriate hospital areas. 3. Well-maintained and -operated ventilation systems. 4. Effective control measures during construction. 5. Windows that open.		

EBD PRINCIPLE 2: Improve the quality and safety of healthcare delivery (continued)

	EBD Repsonses and Features	Present	Comment
Reduce infections spread through contact	1. Single-patient rooms easier to decontaminate. 2. Support handwashing with conveniently placed sinks, handwashing liquid dispensers, and alcohol rubs. 3. Careful selection of materials with cleanability a key consideration. 4. Frequent cleaning of high-contact surfaces.		
Prevent waterborne infections	1. Regular maintenance and inspection of water-supply system to minimize stagnation and back flow and for temperature control. 2. Use proper water treatment. 3. Regularly clean and maintain faucet aerators to prevent and control for Legionella. 4. Avoid decorative water fountains in high-risk patient areas. 5. Fountain water temperature should be kept cold, and fountains should be regularly cleaned and maintained.		
Reduce medication errors	1. Assess adequacy of lighting levels in staff work areas. 2. Provide high lighting levels (1,500 lux) for complex visual tasks. 3. Provide private space for work.		
Reduce room transfers	1. Provide acuity-adaptable rooms. 2. Provide larger patient zone to support more in-room procedures.		
Prevent patient falls	1. Single-patient rooms. 2. Decentralize support in pods. 3. Bed alarms. 4. Assistive devices (for example, headwall rails, larger bathroom doors, bathroom location).		

EBD PRINCIPLE 2: Improve the quality and safety of healthcare delivery (continued)

	EBD Repsonses and Features	Present	Comment
Reduce noise stress. Improve speech intelligibility	1. Single-patient rooms. 2. Install high-performance sound-absorbing acoustical ceiling tiles. 3. Remove or reduce loud noise sources through use of noiseless paging and alarm systems, equipment placement, etc. 4. Provide patient examination rooms and treatment areas with walls that extend fully to the support ceiling. 5. Use carpet and rubber floors where appropriate.		

EBD PRINCIPLE 3: Support care of the whole person, enhanced by contact with nature and positive distractions

	EBD Repsonses and Features	Present	Comment
Decrease patient stress	1. Provide secure access to nature (for example, central green zones). 2. Provide positive distractions (for example, art, music, etc.). 3. Provide multiple spiritual spaces and haven areas. 4. Explore Fisher-house-like support and child-care options. 5. Establish a Patient and Family Design Review Committee.		

EBD PRINCIPLE 4: Create a positive work environment

	EBD Repsonses and Features	Present	Comment
Decrease back pain and work-related injuries	1. Install ceiling-mounted lifts. 2. Use softer floors. 3. Ergonomically evaluate work areas. 4. Provide on-site staff exercise facilities.		
Reduce staff fatigue and increase time with patients	1. Decentralize staff support spaces (such as, charting, supplies, medications) proximate to patient rooms (pod configuration) to minimize staff walking and increase time with patients. 2. Provide windows in staff break rooms so staff has access to natural light.		
Increase healthcare team effectiveness through improved communication	1. Provide different types of spaces for interactive team work. 2. Flexible work spaces. 3. Visual connections to facilitate information seeking and interaction.		
Eliminate noisy chaotic environments	1. See EBD principle #2, reduce noise and consider work flows in relation to key spaces. 2. Provide adequate space for private work to minimize distractions and interruptions. 3. Provide a visual connection to patients.		

EBD PRINCIPLE 5: Design for maximum standardization and future flexibility and growth

	EBD Repsonses and Features	Present	Comment
Facilitate care coordination and patient service.	1. Collocate related services into care centers (for example, musculoskeletal, cancer). 2. Flexible work spaces to encourage multidisciplinary use.		
Expand public space utility.	1. Create flexible public spaces to support multiple missions (for example, Mass-cal, health fairs).		

■■ APPENDIX C:
ANSWERS TO CHAPTER QUESTIONS

Chapter One Review Questions with Answers

1. What are the seven current trends influencing healthcare in the United States today?
   - public focus on quality and patient safety
   - healthcare costs and reimbursment
   - aging population and caregiver shortages
   - health information technology
   - genomics and technology
   - disaster preparedness and emergency room saturation
   - environmental safety and sustainability

2. How can EBD positively influence the challenges represented by these trends?

   EBD can positively influence these challenges by designing healing and therapeutic environments that help reduce errors, improve patient and staff satisfaction, enhance efficiency, and support the latest technological advances, such as HIT and genomics.

Chapter One Quiz Questions with Answers

1. Select the best answer: Evidence-Based Design is the process of basing decisions about _____ on credible research to achieve the best possible outcomes.
   - a. patient outcomes
   - **b. the built environment**
   - c. nursing staff to patient ratios

2. Which one of the following clinical and safety outcomes are typically NOT affected by the design of the physical healthcare environment?

    a. medical errors

    b. adverse reactions to drugs

    c. hospital-associated infections

3. The goal of the business case for EBD is to determine how healthcare facility investments contribute to improvements in patient care quality and the safety and satisfaction of both patients and staff while positively enhancing _____.

    a. the bottom line

    b. the physical design

    c. workforce efficiency

4. To make the business case for physical design innovations, what needs to be balanced against ongoing operating savings and revenue enhancements?

    a. patient outcomes

    b. one-time construction costs

    c. longer design and construction timelines

Chapter Two Review Questions with Answers

1. What are the six typical classifications for inpatient hospitals?

    • ownership

    • length of stay

    • type of service

    • public access

    • location

    • size

2. What are five other types of inpatient hospitals?
   - teaching or academic hospitals
   - critical access hospitals
   - doctor-owned specialty hospitals
   - healthcare systems
   - healthcare networks

3. Name three types of hospital-based outpatient services.
   Any of the following are possible answers:
   - clinical services
   - surgical services
   - women's health centers
   - emergency services
   - home healthcare centers

4. Name two types of free-standing facilities.
   Any of the following are possible answers:
   - walk-in clinics
   - urgent-care centers and emerge-centers
   - surgicenters
   - mobile, medical, diagnostic, and screening services
   - emergency medical technicians

5. List the nine key stakeholders in healthcare facilities.
   1. board of trustees and leadership
   2. researchers and designers
   3. vendors/suppliers
   4. patients
   5. caregivers/family/visitors
   6. staff
   7. community partners
   8. community organizations
   9. donors

6. Why is it important to consider the perspective(s) of hospital staff when designing a healthcare facility?

Staff can provide insight into the design of effective and efficient facilities based on their day-to-day experience of what does and does not work. For example, housekeeping staff are intimately aware of what colors and textures show dirt easily and wear prematurely, while clinical staff can provide input about the effective layout of supply and equipment spaces, work-surface heights and locations, as well as actual care provision areas; IT staff can help forecast space requirements for future equipment needs.

7. Why is it important to consider the perspective(s) of community-based organizations or associations in the design of a healthcare facility?

Many associations are in a position to provide expert advice for the care of their constituencies. For example, the National Association of the Deaf (NAD) is available to consult on design interventions that help to accommodate the needs of the hearing impaired. Public institutions such as libraries, historical societies, and disaster committees can also provide important insights that benefit facility design.

8. Which professionals might comprise a hospital design research team?

A research team may include individuals with research degrees, students, or those with experience in research related to the built environment. Other key members of a research team may include the hospital's quality improvement, records, finance, and information systems managers, as well as clinicians who will aid in identifying, tracking, and monitoring clinical and financial indicators significant to the project goals.

9. What are the six components that make up the Environment of Care (EOC)?

• delivery of care model (concepts)
• facility and service users (people)
• systems design

- layout and operational planning
- physical environment
- design process and implementation

Chapter Two Quiz Questions with Answers

1. Facilities that give patients a wide range of healthcare choices and attempt to meet consumer needs of convenience and cost reduction are collectively known as _____.
   a. walk-in clinics
   b. surgicenters
   c. freestanding facilities

2. _____ refers to any personal care or assistance that a patient receives on an ongoing basis because of a disability or chronic illness that limits his or her ability to function.
   a. long-term care
   b. institutional care
   c. home health care

3. Hospital-based outpatient services can be broadly classified into five main types: clinical, surgical, emergency, home health, and _____ health.
   a. psychiatric
   b. women's
   c. pediatric

4. Outpatient services are also referred to as _____ care.
   a. ambulatory
   b. walk-in
   c. non-institutional

5. Preliminary studies by the Weill Cornell Medical College's Physician Organization in six existing ambulatory sites found that the more attractive the environment, the _____ the perceived quality and the _____ the anxiety.

    a. higher, higher

    b. lower, lower

    c. higher, lower

6. Hospital boards are ultimately accountable for organizational activity, accomplishment, and _____.

    a. staff satisfaction

    b. patient outcomes

    c. major capital investments

7. Who is accountable for all of the services and behaviors of a hospital's organization.

    a. the board chair

    b. the entire board

    c. the CEO

8. Who recommends expenditures to further enable the healthcare facility to meet community needs and/or shareholder value? Who approve(s) or disapprove(s) the recommendation.

    a. board, CEO

    b. CEO, board

    c. CEO, government

9. Which strategy applied to facility design calls for staff involvement in the design of effective and efficient facilities based on their day-to-day experience?

    a. total quality management

    b. universal design

    c. participative management

10. A facility's Environment of Care defines its _____.

   a. physical design

   b. culture

   c. outcomes

Chapter Three Review Questions with Answers

1. How is *research* defined in the context of evidence-based design?

   In evidence-based design, *research* generally refers to empirical research, the systematic investigation of the tangible facts (for example, empirical data) aimed at gaining knowledge, making discoveries, testing or revising theories, and applying the new knowledge. Empirical data refers to the information that can be directly sensed (seen, heard, touched, tasted, and smelled) and is demonstrable to other people.

2. How can existing data within a healthcare facility be used in EBD, given institutional approval?

   Given institutional approval, this database of information may be mined to explore how changes to the built environment relate to health, performance, satisfaction, and economic outcomes.

3. Strong evidence has confirmed that certain design characteristics impact patient and staff outcomes in four key areas. What are these key areas?

   • reduction in staff stress and fatigue

   • improvement in patient safety

   • reduction in patient stress

   • improvement in overall healthcare quality

4. What are three sources for relevant data within the healthcare organizations itself?

   • Measurements of the environment of care (EOC), including the daily changes in temperature, light, sound, location, dimension, distance, materials, furnishings, or equipment used in the care setting.

- Measures on health status routinely collected by the facility
- Survey data

5. In what ways can the research process improve communication among team members?

Research can improve communication by providing a common language between stakeholders, help designers to effectively communicate with owners over competing design options, and help resolve possible disagreements.

Chapter Three Quiz Questions with Answers

1. The EBD process is differentiated from the typical design process because it _____.

   a. involves staff in design decision making

   b. uses research to develop and evaluate design innovations

   c. changes the composition of the interdisciplinary design team

2. Ideally, EBD research can be used during and after the construction and occupancy phases to _____.

   a. develop hypotheses about how the design decisions may impact outcomes

   b. evaluate the effectiveness of design solutions

   c. alter parts of the design as it becomes clear whether or not decisions were appropriate

3. At which phase of the project should stakeholders use research to understand which environmental elements are the best design options to improve outcomes?

   a. predesign/design

   b. construction

   c. occupancy

4. Specific information about the built environment recorded over time and relative to patient and staff exposure during their time within that setting is needed to assert _____ relationships between features of the built environment and outcomes.

    a. theoretical

    b. correlational

    c. causal

Chapter Four Review Questions with Answers

1. List the key steps in an EBD process.

- Define evidence-based goals and objectives.
- Find sources for relevant evidence.
- Critically interpret relevant evidence.
- Create and innovate evidence-based design concepts.
- Develop a hypothesis.
- Collect baseline performance measures.
- Monitor implementation of design and construction.
- Measure post-occupancy performance results.

2. What is the value of conducting visioning sessions with key patient, staff, and community members when launching the project?

They clarify the project message, image, brand, or theme, as well as identify desired features or amenities and services to be included in the project.

Chapter Four Quiz Questions with Answers

1. The EBD process can be integrated into _____ stage of the building design process.

    a. the predesign/design

    b. the construction

    c. any

2. The phase when the building is outfitted with everything needed to make it ready for patient care services is called the _____.

   a. programming phase

   b. commissioning phase

   c. occupancy phase

acuity: The intensity of care necessary to meet the needs of a patient.

adverse drug events (ADES): Generally unwanted, negative consequences associated with the use of given medications.

asclepieion: A healing temple sacred to the god Asclepius in ancient Greece. In the 6th century BC, an asclepieion intuitively placed patient rooms with an orientation to the sun.

board of trustees: The governing body of an organization or corporation that is generally elected by stakeholders to make decisions and policies.

built environment: Manmade surroundings where human activity occurs.

business planning: Determining the strategies, goals and objectives of the business by translating the current and strategic state in terms of costs and revenues with regard to investments.

commissioning: The process of outfitting the building with the equipment and furniture not included as built-in features during construction.

credible research: The believable and convincing study of a subject or topic to discover new information and understanding through reliable and defendable sources.

emergicenters: Care centers that are open 24 hours a day, 7 days a week, and accept patients with no appointments. They provide a wide range of routine services for basic and acute conditions on a first-come, first-serve basis.

evidence-based design (EBD): The process of basing decisions about the built environment on credible research to achieve the best possible outcomes.

Environment of Care (EOC): The understanding that the experience one has in a healthcare delivery system is a function of six components: physical environment, layout and operations, systems, people, concepts, and implementation.

facility master plan: Sometimes referred to as the facility portfolio. A document that describes an overall physical development concept through maps and narrative.

Failure Modes and Effects Analysis (FMEA): Provides a safety evaluation tool when reviewing emerging project design documents.

genomics: The study of genes and their implementation in the development of healthcare products and services.

health maintenance organizations (HMOs): A type of managed care that provides healthcare coverage; most require a primary care physician.

healthcare delivery system: Refers to all facilities and services that provide health care.

hospital-associated infections (HAIs): An infection acquired in the hospital by a patient who was admitted for a reason other than that infection. This includes infections acquired in the hospital, but appearing after discharge, as well as occupational infections among facility staff.

long-term care: Refers to any personal care or assistance an individual might receive on a long-term basis because of a disability or chronic illness that limits his or her ability to function.

managed care: An individual or group insurance plan that includes health maintenance organizations (HMO) and preferred provider organizations (PPO).

meta-analysis: A quantitative, statistical analysis of experiments or studies which analyzes the collective data for statistical meaning.

occupancy: Represents the act of moving to full functional residency in a new facility or space.

operations: Begins with post-occupancy EBD evaluations and represents the routine maintenance and repair activities necessary to keep the building in good working order over the life of the building.

outcomes: The target goals for a healthcare organization, many being linked to the built environment.

outpatient services: Also referred to as ambulatory care.

Constitutes diagnostic and therapeutic services and treatments provided to the walking (ambulatory) patient and do not constitute an overnight stay.

patient: The person seeking healthcare service in the healthcare industry.

pay for performance: Refers to a method to foster quality performance by providing pay incentives or bonuses for quality work.

peer-reviewed journals: A scholarly periodical which requires each article submitted for publication be reviewed and assessed by an independent panel of experts.

performance-based building (PBB): Specifies particular materials or designs that a building must include to achieve a targeted performance level.

physical environment: Refers to the external, tangible surroundings which can influence behavior and development.

preferred provider organization (PPO): An organization providing health insurance coverage that encourages participants to visit certain physicians, laboratories, and hospitals at a decreased rate.

primary care: Coordinates the delivery of health services between the patient and various delivery components, which includes both preventative and curative, over a period of time to coordinate all the care a patient receives. Regarded as essential healthcare.

process: A set method of doing something involving ordered steps or operations.

programming: An American Institute of Architects guideline updated every four years, which reflects a number of Design strategies. Programming, along with other research, helps determine the number and size of rooms to support the described concept of operations for each area in the hospital.

project planning: A detailed concept of operations for each clinical or administrative area.

randomized controlled trials (RCT): Quantitative, comparative, controlled experiments in which researchers study two or more interventions in a series of persons who receive them in a random order.

research: The systematic investigation and study of a topic or idea, based on empirical data, aimed at gaining knowledge, making discoveries, testing new theories, and applying the new knowledge.

return on investment (ROI): A framework that represents the common tool used by chief financial officers to financially evaluate major investment decisions in terms of cost and revenue.

sociotechnical theory: Refers to the relationship between social and technical aspects of an organization, usually based on designing different kinds of organizations where the relationship between socio and technical elements lead to the emergence of productivity and wellbeing.

stakeholders: Those with a vested interest in a project or those involved at the implementation of the project that care about its success.

strategic planning: A top-down approach concerned with the mission and long-term objectives of an organization.

transition planning: An additional phase in the Facility Life Cycle Model that ensures that all the necessary steps are planned and implemented to successfully move the organization from its present state to the envisioned future.

universal healthcare: Healthcare coverage that is extended to all residents of a governmental region.

users: In EBD, those whom the physical environment was created for, including patients, their families, staff, and others.

visioning: The process of developing, identifying, and documenting the values of an organization or project through a written vision statement.

Related Organizations Referenced in Study Guide One

American Hospital Association (AHA)
www.americanheart.org

American Institute of Architects (AIA)
www.aia.org

Bronson Methodist Hospital
www.bronsonhealth.com

Center for Disease Control and Prevention (CDC)
www.cdc.gov

The Center for Health Design (CHD)
www.healthdesign.org

Center for Studying Health System Change
www.hschange.com

Centers for Medicare and Medicaid Services (CMS)
www.cms.hhs.gov

The Children's Hospital
www.thechildrenshospital.org

Cochrane Collaboration
www.cochrane.org

Commonwealth Fund Commission
www.commonwealthfund.org

Cornell University
www.cornell.edu

Department of Health and Human Services (HHS)
www.hhs.gov

Hospital Compare
www.hospitalcompare.hhs.gov

The Institute for Healthcare Improvement (IHI)
www.ihi.org

Institute of Medicine (IOM)
www.iom.edu

Internal Revenue Service
www.irs.gov

Joint Commission
www.jointcommission.org

Military Health System (MHS)
www.health.mil

Modern Healthcare
www.modernhealthcare.com

National Quality Forum
www.qualityforum.org

Palomar Pomerado Health
www.pph.org

Planetree
www.planetree.org

Press Ganey
www.pressganey.com

Robert Wood Johnson Foundation
www.rwjf.org

St. Joseph's Community Hospital
www.newstjosephs.com

US General Services Administration
www.gsa.gov

Veteran's Administration
www.va.gov

■ REFERENCES

American Hospital Association. (2010). *Fast facts on US hospitals*. Retrieved from www.aha.org/aha/resource-center/Statistics-and-Studies/fast-facts.html

American Medical Associate. (2010). American recovery and re-investment act of 2009 (ARRA). Retrieved from www.ama-assn.org/ama/pub/advocacy/current-topics-advocacy/hr1-stimulus-summary.shtml

American Institute of Architects (AIA). (2006). Guidelines for Design and Construction of Health Care Facilities. Dallas, TX: Facility Guidelines Institute.

Arnon, S., Shapsam A., Forman, L., Regev, R., Bauer, S., Lit-manovitz, I., & Dolfin, T. (2006). Live music is beneficial to preterm infants in the neonatal intensive care unit environment. *Birth, 33*(2), 131-136.

Appelbaum, S. H. (1997). Socio-technical systems theory: An intervention strategy for organizational development. *Management Decision, 35*(6), 452-363.

Arizona Hospital and Healthcare Association. (2006, August 25). Bush launches healthcare transparency initiative. *Arizona Hospital and Healthcare Association Weekly Newsletter.*

Aspinall, M., & Hamermesh, R. G. (2007, October). Realizing the promise of personalized medicine, *Harvard Business Review*, 109-117.

Austin, A., & Wetle, V. (2008). *The United States health care system*. Upper Saddle River, NJ: Pearson Prentice Hall.

Baird, G., Gray, J., Isaacs, N., Kernohan, D., & McIndoe, G. (Eds.). (1996). *Building evaluation techniques.* New York: McGraw-Hill.

Beaudoin, J. (2007, November 20). Massachusetts hospitals make "no charge" pledge for adverse events. *Healthcare Finance News.* Retrieved from http://www.healthcarefinancenews.com/news/massachusetts-hospitals-make-no-charge-pledge-adverse-events

Becker, F., & Jones-Douglass, S. (2008). The ecology of the patient visit: Physical attractiveness, waiting times, and perceived quality of care. *Journal of Ambulatory Care Management, 31*(2), 124-137.

Berry, L., Parker, D., Coile, R., Hamilton, D.K., O'Neil, D., & Sadler, B. (2004). The business case for better buildings. *Frontiers in Health Service Management. 21*(1), 3-21.

Brainard, G. C., Hanifin, J. P., Rollag, M. D., Greeson, J., Byrne, B., Glickman, G., … Sanford, B. (2001). Human melatonin regulation is not mediated by the three cone photooptic visual system. *The Journal of Clinical Endocrinology and Metabolism, 86*(1), 433-6.

Bronson Methodist Hospital. (March 29, 2010). Bronson Methodist Hospital Named One of the Nation's 100 Top Hospitals. *Bronson Methodist Press Release.* Retrieved from www.bronsonhealth.com/WhatsNew/page5285.html

Caldwell, D. F., Chatman, J., O'Reilly, C. A., Ormiston, M., & Lapitz, M. (2008, April/June). Implementing strategic change in a health care system: The importance of leadership and change readiness. *Health Care Management Review, 33*(2), 124-133.

Carpman, J., & Grant, M. (1993). *Design that cares: Planning health facilities for patients and visitors* (2nd ed.). Chicago, IL: Josey-Bass American Hospital Association Press.

Carver, J. (2006). Boards that make a difference. *J-B Carver Board Governance Series.* San Francisco, CA: Jossey-Bass.

Casscells, S.W., Kurmel, T., & Ponatoski, E. (2009). Creating healing environments in support of the U.S. military: A commitment to quality through the built environment. *Health Environments Research and Design Journal, 2*(2), 134–145.

Cassidy, R. (2003, November 1). *Building Design and Construction Magazine.* White paper. Retrieved from www.bdcnetwork.com/

Centers for Medicare and Medicaid Services. (2007). *Hospital care quality information from the consumer perspective.* Retrieved from www.hcahpsonline.org/default.aspx

Centers for Disease Control and Prevention. (2008). *Avian influenza.* Retrieved from www.cdc.gov/flu/avian/outbreaks/current.htm

Centers for Disease Control and Prevention. (2008). *Estimates for healthcare associated infections.* Retrieved from www.cdc.gov/ncidod/dhqp/hai.html

The Center for Health Design (CHD). (2008a). *Pebble project.* Retrieved from www.healthdesign.org/research/pebble/

The Center for Health Design. (2008b). *Evidence-based design definition.* Retrieved from www.healthdesign.org/blog/

The Center for Health Design. (2007). *Evidence-based design accreditation and certification (EDAC): Base knowledge documents.* Unpublished paper.

The Commonwealth Fund. (April 1, 2010). *Timeline for health care reform implementation: Health insurance provisions.* New York, NY: The Commonwealth Fund.

Chaudhry, B, Wang, J., Wu, S., Maglione, M., Mojica, W., Roth, E., ... S.C., Shekelle, P.G. (2006). Systematic review of health information technology on quality, efficiency, and costs of medical care. *Annals of Internal Medicine, 144*(10), 742-752.

Clipson, C. W., & Johnson, R. E. (1987). Integrated approaches to facilities planning and assessment. *Planning for Higher Education, 15*(3), 12-22.

Clipson, C. W., & Wehrer, J. J. (1973). *Planning for cardiac care: A guide to the planning and design of cardiac care facilities.* Ann Arbor, MI: Health Administration Press.

Cochrane, A. L. (1972). *Effectiveness and efficiency: Random reflections on health services.* London: The Nuffield Provincial Hospitals Trust.

Cohen, J. D. (2006). The aging nursing workforce: How to retain experienced nurses. *Journal of Healthcare Management, 51*(4), 233-245.

The Commonwealth Fund Commission on a High Performance Health System. (2006, September). *Why not the best? Results from a national scorecard on U.S. health system performance, 2008.* Retrieved from http://www.commonwealthfund.org/Content/Publications/Fund-Reports/2008/Jul/Why-Not-the-Best--Results-from-the-National-Scorecard-on-U-S--Health-System-Performance--2008.aspx

Colmers, J. (2007, January). *Public reporting and transparency*. Prepared for The Commonwealth Fund/Alliance for Health Reform 2007 Bipartisan Congressional Health Policy Conference.

Cutler, R., Rosen, A.B., & Vijan, S. (2006, August 31). The value of medical spending in the United States, 1960-2000. *The New England Journal of Medicine, 355*(9), 920-927.

DoBias, M. (2006, March 20). Lifting the lid off of pricing. *Modern Healthcare*. Chicago, IL.

Edelstein, E. A., Ellis, R. J., Sollers, J. J., III, Chong, G., Brandt, R., & Thayer, J. F. (2006, October). *The effects of lighting on autonomic control of the heart*. Presented at the Society for Psychophysiological Research 47th Annual Meeting, Savannah, GA.

Energy Information Administration. (2010). *Principal building activities in the commercial buildings energy consumption survey (CBECS)*. Retrieved from www.eia.doe.gov/emeu/consumption briefs/cbecs/pbawebsite/contents.htm

Facilities Guidelines Institute. (2010). *Guidelines for the design and construction of health care facilities*, (2010 ed.). Dallas, TX.

Figueiro, M. G., Rea, M. S., & Bullough, J. D. (2006). Circadian effectiveness of two polychromatic lights in suppressing human nocturnal melatonin. *Neuroscience Letters, 406*(3), 293-297.

Garber, K. M. (Ed.). (2006). *The US healthcare system: Fundamental facts, definitions and statistics*. Chicago, IL: Health Forum, Inc.

Gapenski, L. C. (2007). *Healthcare finance* (4th ed.). Chicago, IL: Health Administration Press.

Georgia Institute of Technology, College of Architecture. (2008, March). *Proceedings: Evidence-based design 2.0 Collaborative Workshop*. Falls Church, VI.

Gifford, R. (1997). *Environmental psychology: Principles and practice (*2nd ed.). Needham Heights, MA: Allyn & Bacon.

Griffith, J. R. & White, K. R. (2007). *The well-managed healthcare organization* (6th ed.). Chicago, IL: Health Administration Press.

Gosfield, A. G., and Reinertsen, J. L. (2005). The 100,000 Lives Campaign: Crystallizing standards of care for hospitals. *Health Affairs, 24*(6), 1560-1570.

Hamilton, D. K. (2003). Four levels of evidence-based practice. *Healthcare Design, 3*, 18-26.

Hamilton, D. K. (2004). The four levels of evidence-based practice. *AIA Journal of Architecture.* Retrieved from http://www.arch.ttu.edu/courses/2007/fall/5395/392/students/garay/Research/Research.pdf

Hamilton, D. K. & Orr, R. (2006). Cultural transformation and design. In S.O. Marberry (Ed.), *Improving healthcare with better building design,* (pp. 145-160). Ann Arbor, MI: Health Administration Press.

Hamilton, D. K., Orr, R., & Raboin, W. E. (2008). Organizational transformation: A model for joint optimization of culture change and evidence-based design. *Health Education, Research and Design. 1*(3), 40-60.

Hatcher, B. (Ed). (2006). *Wisdom at work: The importance of the older and experienced nurse in the workplace.* Retrieved from http://www.rwjf.org/pr/product.jsp?id=43408

Haughey, J. (2010). Healthcare entitlement will not boost health-care construction. Reed Construction Data. Retrieved from www.reedconstructiondata.com/jim-haughey/post/healthcare-entitlement-will-not-boost-healthcare-construction/

HealthGrades. (2008).The fifth annual healthgrades patient safety in American hospitals study. Retrieved from www.health grades.com/media/dms/pdf/patientsafetyinamericanhospitals study2008.pdf

HealthLeaders Media. (2010). Overall cross-sector survey. Retrieved from www.healthleadersmedia.com/industry_survey/

Health Systems Resources. (2008). World health statistics 2008: Global health indicators. World Health Organization. Retrieved from www.who.int/whois/whostat/EN_WHS08_table4_HSR.pdf

Henriksen, K., Isaacson, S., Sadler, B. L., & Zimring, C. M. (2007). The role of the physical environment in crossing the quality chasm. *Joint Commission Journal on Quality and Patient Safety*, *33*(11), 68-80.

Hensing, J., Dahlen, D., Warden, M., Van Norman, J., Wilson, B. C., & Kisiel, S. (2008). Measuring the benefits of IT-enabled care transformation. *Healthcare Financial Management*, *2*, 74-80.

Hickey, J. V. & Casner-Lotto, J. (1998). How to get true employee participation. *Training and Development, 52*, 58-61.

Horan, T. C., Andrus, M., Dudeck, M. A., (2008). The Center for Disease Control and Prevention/NHSN. *America Journal of Infection Control, 36*(5), 309-32.

Institute for Healthcare Improvement. (2005). Going lean in healthcare. IHI Innovation series white paper. Cambridge, MA: Institute for Healthcare Improvement.

Institute for Healthcare Improvement. (2008). *100,000 Lives Campaign*. Retrieved from www.ihi.org/IHI/Programs?Campaign/Campaign.htm?Tabld=1

Institute for Healthcare Improvement. (2010). Campaign results and what's next: Has the 5 million lives campaign ended? Retrieved from www.ihi.org/IHI/Programs/Campaign/Campaign.htm?TabId=6

Institute of Medicine. (2000). *To err is human: Building a safer health system.* Washington, DC: National Academies Press.

Institute of Medicine. (2001). *Crossing the quality chasm: A new health system for the 21ˢᵗ century.* Washington, DC: National Academies Press.

Institute of Medicine. (2003). *Priority areas for national action: transforming healthcare quality.* Adams, K & Corrigan, J. M. (Eds.). Washington, DC: National Academies Press.

Institute of Medicine. (2004). *Keeping patients safe: Transforming the work environment of nurses.* Washington, DC: National Academies Press.

Institute of Medicine. (2007). *IOM quality aims.* Washington, DC: National Academies Press.

Joint Commission Resources. (2005). *Infection control issues in the environment of care: Improving health care quality and safety.* Miller, K. M., (Ed). Joint Commission Resources, Inc.

The Joint Commission. (2010). *National patient safety goals.* Retrieved from www.jointcommission.org/PatientSafety/ NationalPatientSafetyGoals/

Jones, H. (2009). FMI's construction outlook – third quarter 2009. Raleigh, NC: FMI.

Joseph, A., & Fritz, L. (2006). Ceiling lifts reduce patient-handling injuries. *Healthcare Design, 6*, 10-13.

Kaiser Family Foundation. (2007). *Snapshots: Health care costs.* Retrieved from www.kff.org/insurance/snapshot

Kotter, J. P., & Heskett, J. L. (1992). *Corporate culture and performance.* New York: The Free Press.

Lounsbury, M. (2003). On Location: Green Build 2003. *Sustainable Industries Journal.* Retrieved from www.greenerbuildings. com/news_detial.cfm?newsID=26214

Malone, E. B., Mann-Dooks, J. R., & Strauss, J. (2007). *Evidence-based design: Application in the MHS.* Falls Church, VA: Noblis.

Medical Architecture Research Unit. (1971). *Reduced bed spacing in hospital wards.* London: Faculty of Engineering, Science and the Built Environment, London South Bank University.

Medical Architecture Research Unit. (1973a). *First phase of an investigation into the education and training needs of health facility planners.* London: Faculty of Engineering, Science and the Built Environment, London South Bank University.

Medical Architecture Research Unit. (1973b). *Health centers handbook.* London: Faculty of Engineering, Science and the

Built Environment, London South Bank University.

Medical Architecture Research Unit. (1976). *The development of a classification framework for selecting case study hospitals.* London: Faculty of Engineering, Science and the Built Environment, London South Bank University.

Medical Architecture Research Unit. (1977). *Space unitization in hospitals: Concepts, methodology and preliminary results.* London: Faculty of Engineering, Science and the Built Environment, London South Bank University.

National Association of Children's Hospitals and Related Institutions in collaboration with The Center for Health Design. (2008). *Evidence for innovation: Transforming children's health through the physical environment.* Alexandria: VI: National Association of Children's Hospitals and Related Institutions.

National Quality Forum. (2006). *Serious reportable events in healthcare: 2005-2006 update.* Retrieved from www.qualityforum.org/projects/completed/sre/

Nelson, R. (2006). Designing to heal: A new trend in evidence-based, nurse-friendly hospital design. *American Journal of Nursing, 106*(11), 25-27.

Nelson, V. (2008). Blending old and new to achieve the extraordinary. *Healthcare Design.* Retrieved from www.healthcare designmagazine.com/ME2/dirmod.asp?sid=9B6FFC4 46FF7486981EA3C0C3CCE4943&nm=Articles&typ e=Publishing&mod=Publications%3A%3AArticle&mi d=8F3A7027421841978F18BE895F87F791&tier=4&i d=90FC8157983F40F29448CBC31E9475AF

Neumann, P., Palmer, J., Daniels, D., Quigley, K., Gold, M., & Chao, S. (2008). A strategic plan for integrating cost-effectiveness analysis into the US healthcare system, *The American Journal of Managed Care, 14*(4), 185-188.

Oregon State Web site. (2010). *What is a safety net?* Retrieved from www.oregon.gov/DHS/ph/bcc/docs/safety_net_definition.pdf

Ossmann, M., Dellinger, B., Boenecke, C. (2008). Healing environments for America's heroes. *Healthcare Design, 8*(11), 28-38.

The Oxford English Dictionary (4ᵗʰ ed.). (2000). Oxford, England: Oxford University Press.

Page, A. (2004). *Keeping patients safe: Transforming the work environment of nurses.* Washington DC: Institute of Medicine of the National Academics.

Partnerships British Columbia. (2010). Understanding public private partnerships. Retrieved from www.partnershipsbc.ca/pdf/Understanding%20Public%20Private%20Partnerships%2023-mar-06.pdf

Practice Greenhealth. (2010). *Water conservation.* Retrieved from cms.h2e-online.org/ee/facilities/waterconserve/

Practice Greenhealth. (2010). *Waste Reduction.* Retrieved from cms.h2e-online.org/ee/waste-reduction/

Purser, R. E., & Cabana, S. (1997). Involve employees at every level of strategic planning. *Quality Progress, 30*(5), 66-71.

Ranji, S. R., Shetty, K., Posley, K.A., Lewis, R., Sundaram, V., Galvin, C. M., Winston, L. G. (2007). Prevention of healthcare-associated infections. In Shojania, K.G., McDonald, K.M., Wachter R.M., Owens, D.K. (Eds). *Closing the Quality Gap: A critical analysis of quality improvement strategies.* AHRQ Publication No. 04(07)-0051-6. Rockville, MD: Agency for Healthcare Research and Quality.

Regnier, V. (1994). Assisted living housing for the elderly: Design innovations from the United States and Europe. New York: Van Nostrand Reinhold.

Reiling, J. (2007). *Safe by design: Designing safety in health care facilities, process and culture.* Oak Brook, IL: Joint Commission Resource, Inc.

Roberts, G., & Guenther, R. (2006). Environmentally responsible hospitals in *Improving Healthcare with Better Building Design.* Chicago, IL: Health Administration Press.

Rodriguez, H., & Aguirre, B. E. (2006). Hurricane Katrina and the healthcare infrastructure: A focus on disaster preparedness, response and resiliency. *Frontiers of Health Services Management, 23*(1),13-25.

Rollins, J. A., (2004). Evidence-based hospital design improves health care outcomes for patients, families and staff. *Pediatric Nursing, 30*(4), 338.

Rubin, H., Owens, A. J., & Golden, G. (1998). Status report: An investigation to determine whether the built environment affects patients' medication outcomes. Concord, CA: The Center for Health Design.

Sackett, D. L., Rosenberg, W., Gray, J. A. M., Haynes, R. B., & Richardson, W. S. (1996). Evidenced based medicine: What it is and what it is not. *British Medical Journal, 312,* 71-72.

Sadler, B. (2009). Letter to the editor. *Health Environment Research and Design Journal, 3*(1), 102-104.

Sadler, B., DuBose, J., & Zimring, C. (2008). The business case for building better hospitals through evidence based design. *Healthcare Environments Research & Design Journal, 1*(3), 22-39.

Sadler, B., DuBose, J., Malone, E., & Zimring, C. (2008). *The business case for building better hospitals through evidence-based design.* Concord, CA: The Center for Health Design.

Scott, R. D. (2009). The direct medical costs of healthcare-associated infections in U.S. hospitals and the benefits of prevention. Atlanta, GA: Centers for Disease Control and Prevention.

Schein, E. H. (1992). *Organizational culture and leadership* (2nd ed.). San Francisco, CA: Jossey-Bass.

Schein, E. H. (2004). *Organizational culture and leadership.* San Francisco, CA: Jossey-Bass.

Schoen, C., How, S.K.H., Weinbaum, I. Greg, J. E., Jr., & Davis, K. K. (2006). Public views on shaping the future of the US health system. *The Commonwealth Fund,* August 2006. Retrieved July 22, 2008 from http://www.commonwealth fund.org/Content/Publications/Fund-Reports/2006/Aug/Public-Views-on-Shaping-the-Future-of-the-U-S--Health-System.aspx

Sommer, R., & Sommer, B. B. (2002). *A practical guide to behavioral research: tools and techniques* (5th ed.). New York, NY: Oxford University Press.

Stichler, J. F. (2009). Scientific writing, peer review, and turning lemons into lemonade. *Health Environments Research and Design Journal, 2*(2), 70-72.

Stichler, J. F., & Hamilton, K. D. (2008). Evidence-based design: What is it? *Health Environments Research and Design, 1*(2), 3-4.

Stone, S., (2008). A retrospective evaluation of the impact of the Planetree patient-centered model of care on inpatient quality outcomes. *Health Environments Research and Design Journal, 1*(4), 55-69.

Synergy Health Foundation Pathway. (2004). St. Joseph's West Bend foundation newsletter, October 2004. Retrieved from www.stjosephswb.com/documents%2Foundation%2FPathways%20Oct%202004%2Epdf

Ulrich, R. S. (1984). A view through a window may influence recovery from surgery. *Science, 224*(4647), 420-421.

Ulrich, R.S. & Zimring, C. (2008). The state of evidence-based design research. Presented at the Healthcare Design Conference, Washington, D.C.

Ulrich, R. S., & Zimring, C., Joseph, A., Quan, X., Choudhury, B. (2004). *The role of the physical environment in the hospital of the 21st century: A once-in-a-lifetime opportunity.* Concord, CA: The Center for Health Design.

Ulrich, R. S., Zimring, C., Zhu, X., DuBose, J., Seo, H., Choi, Y., ... Joseph, A., (2008). A review of the scientific literature on evidence-based healthcare design. *Healthcare Environments Research & Design Journal, 1*(3), 61-125.

US Army Health Facility Planning Agency. (1996). Facility life cycle management model. *USA HFPA Brochure*. Falls Church, VA.

US Department of Energy. (2010). Department of Energy announces the launch of the hospital energy alliance to increase energy efficiency in the healthcare sector. Retrieved from www.energy.gov/news2009/7363.htm

US Department of Energy. (2010, April 29). *Department of Energy announces the launch of the hospital energy alliance to increase energy efficiency in the healthcare sector*, [Press release]. Washington D.C.: US Department of Energy.

US General Services Administration. (2008). Definition of value engineering. Retrieved from www.gsa.gov/portal/gsa/ep/content view.do?contenttype=gsa_overview&contentID=8155&noc=T

US Government Accountability Office. (2006). Health information technology: HHS is continuing efforts to define its national strategy. *Southern California Evidence Based Practice Center*. Retrieved from www.research.microsoft.com/towards2020science

Viets, E. (2009). Lessons from evidence-based medicine: What healthcare designers can learn from the medical field. *Health Environments Research and Design Journal, 2*(2), 73-87.

Watkinson, B. (2008). P3 for you and me? The relatively recent and hotly debated procurement model of public-private partnerships brings both opportunities and risks. *Canadian Architect*. Retrieved from www.canadianarchitect.com/issues/story.aspx?aid=1000221446

Webster's Dictionary (2nd college ed). (2000). New York, NY: Random House, Inc.

Wikipedia. (2010). Health information technology. Retrieved from en.wikipedia.org/wiki/Health_information_technology

Wikipedia. (2010). Public-private partnership. Retrieved from en.wikipedia.org/wiki/Public–private_partnership

Wachter, R. M., Foster, N., & Dudley, R. A. (2008). Medicare's decision to withhold payment for hospital errors. *The Joint Commission Journal on Quality and Patient Safety*, *34*(2), 116-123.

Weems, K. (2008). Pay for performance is key to curbing Medicare costs. *AHA News*. Retrieved from www.hospitalconnect.com/ahanews_app/jsp/display.jsp?dcrpath+AHANEWS/AHA

World Health Organization Collaborating Centre for Patient Safety Solutions. (2010). Patient safety solutions. Retrieved from www.ccforpatientsafety.org/patient-safety-solutions/

Zensius, N. (2010). The Center for Health Design's Reality Check: Evidence-based design issues to watch in 2010. *Healthcare Design*, *10*(2), 28-41.

Zensius, N. (2008). Dublin Methodist Hospital: Evidence-based design at work. *Healthcare Design*. Retrieved, from www.healthcaredesignmagazine.com/ME2/dirmod.asp?sid=9B6FFC446FF7486981EA3C0C3CCE4943&nm=Articles&type=Publishing&mod=Publications%3A%3AArticle&mid=8F3A7027421841978F18BE895F87F791&tier=4&id=EBA276D2D1E749E3BCAB06CADA0D2F74

Zimring, C. M., Augenbroe, G., Malone, E. B., & Sadler, B. (2008). Implementing healthcare excellence: The vital role of the CEO in evidence-based design. *Healthcare Environments Research & Design Journal*, *1*(3), 7-8.

Zimring, C. (2002). Post-occupancy evaluation: issues and implementation in T.B. Bechtel & A. Ts'erts'man (Eds.), *Handbook of environmental psychology.* (pp. 306-323). New York: J. Wiley.

AUTHOR BIOGRAPHIES

Phyllis Goetz, PDAC, EDAC

Phyllis Goetz is a vice president for Nurture by Steelcase. Ms. Goetz has over 25 years of healthcare-related experience and is responsible for sales, focused on serving the needs of the architectural and design community and as a liaison with the leading healthcare networks organizations. Ms. Goetz represents Nurture as a Corporate Pebble Partner of The Center for Health Design and serves on committees for Evidence Based Design Accreditation and Certification (EDAC), Rice Building Institute, Health Industry Advisory Council of Texas A&M University, and Planetree Design Advisory. Ms. Goetz frequently speaks at major events. As a member of the Nurture research team she has firsthand knowledge of how healthcare is delivered and how it might be changing in the future.

Eileen B. Malone, RN, MSN, MS, EDAC

Eileen Malone is the senior partner for Mercury Healthcare Consulting, LLC located in Alexandria, Virginia. Ms. Malone supports clients embracing evidence-based design in healthcare facility projects as a means to improve patient, staff, and resource outcomes. Ms. Malone retired from the United States Army at the rank of colonel, after having served as the CIO for the Army Medical Department, a hospital commander/CEO, congressional affairs liaison, facility planner, nurse methods analyst, and nurse practitioner. She currently serves as a member of The Center for Health Design's Research Coalition.

Constance Harmsen, RN, MS, MHA, FACHE, EDAC

Connie Harmsen is chief executive officer of the Surgical Speciality Hospital of Arizona. Ms. Harmsen was also the first chief executive officer for Banner Estrella Medical Center in Phoenix, Arizona, a new 172-bed greenfield site hospital that opened in

January 2005. During her four years as CEO, she was responsible for planning, designing, building, making operational, and opening the "hospital for the future". Banner Estrella received the AIA Honor Award in 2005 and Modern Healthcare's Best of the Best award with the statement: "It is as close to the hospital of the future that exists today." Prior to her role at Banner Estrella, Ms. Harmsen was the Chief Operating Officer at Banner Good Samaritan Medical Center and an administrator with the Presbyterian Health System in Albuquerque, New Mexico and several hospitals in the Midwest. Ms. Harmsen also is a consultant to Starizon, Inc on healthcare design.

Karen (Kathy) Reno, PhD, MBA, RN, EDAC

Ms. Reno serves as a consultant for Joint Commission Resources and Joint Commission International. She is also an assistant clinical professor, coordinator DNP executive leadership concentration at The University of Illinois at Chicago, College of Nursing. Ms. Reno has over 35 years of experience in healthcare, most spent in administrative roles as chief nursing officer for organizations as well as chief operating officer for clinical services. She has been active in many states, national boards and advisory groups. She has lectured on numerous topics including safe facility design, board relations, hospital finances, safety, and technology. She has recently been involved with safe health care facility design with the Ministry of Health for Turkey.

Eve Edelstein, PhD, FAAA, Assoc. AIA, EDAC

Dr. Edelstein bridges both neurobiological and architectural disciplines. She has a doctorate from the University College, London. Dr. Edelstein teaches neuroscience to architects at the NewSchool of Architecture & Design and is a visiting scholar at the University of California, San Diego. Dr. Edelstein works with the Academy of Neuroscience for Architecture to develop their research, professional, and educational programs. She liaisons with the Academy of Architecture for Health, and is a principal investigator for the 2005 AIA Latrobe Fellowship. She directed designs for laboratory improvements at the Salk Institute and educational facilities at San Diego State University. Her work seeks to bring together the database of knowledge offered by psychological, sociological, and physiological disciplines for the benefit of healthcare design.

D. Kirk Hamilton, FAIA, FACHA, EDAC

D. Kirk Hamilton is an associate professor of architecture and associate director of the Center for Health Systems & Design at Texas A&M University. The focus of his academic research is the relationship of evidence-based health facility design to measurable organizational performance. Mr. Hamilton is a board-certified healthcare architect and a founding principal emeritus of WHR Architects, with 30 years of active practice. He is a past president of the American College of Healthcare Architects and the AIA Academy of Architecture for Health. He serves on the board of The Center for Health Design and is co-editor of the new peer-reviewed, interdisciplinary Health Environments Research & Design Journal (HERD).

Alberto Salvatore, AIA, NCARB, EDAC

Alberto Salvatore is co-founder and principal of Salvatore Associates. Mr. Salvatore has over 25 years of experience in healthcare architectural master planning, department planning, programming, and design. In addition to his work defining the evidence-based design process, Mr. Salvatore continues to develop contemporary approaches to achieve the highest quality outcomes for the industry and healthcare leaders. Mr. Salvatore has maintained a commitment to healthcare design through his involvement with The Center for Healthcare Design's Evidence-Based Design Accreditation and Certification (EDAC) program, the Environmental Standards Council (ESC), The Joint Commission Guidelines

Committee, and the Health Guidelines Revision Committee (HGRC) for the *Guidelines for Design and Construction of Health Care Facilities.*

Julie R. Mann-Dooks

Julie Mann-Dooks has 14 years of experience in healthcare consulting. As a part of the Noblis analytical team, she uses her data processing, GIS, and research skills to assist client decision-making in strategic and facility planning. For the last 6 years, Ms. Mann-Dooks has worked primarily on projects for the US Army Health Facility Planning Agency and the TRICARE Management Activity. In 2007 she researched evidence-based design (EBD) and its potential application in the military health system and co-authored a major report on the subject with Ms. Eileen Malone; she has led the EBD tasks for these clients since 2006. Ms. Mann-Dooks graduated *magna cum laude* from Wellesley College in Massachusetts.

Charisse Oland, MHA, RD, FACHE, EDAC

Charisse Oland is the CEO of the Rehabilitation Hospital of Wisconsin, the only freestanding rehab hospital in the state that opened in October 2008. The new facility design is based on a uniquely developed rehab care delivery model—Care at the Patient Side—utilizing healing environment principles to enhance the patient care experience and organizational culture. Ms. Oland has been a healthcare executive for over 25 years, serving as the president of a children's hospital and as a consultant in healthcare organizational development and facility design. Ms. Oland is currently pursuing a doctoral degree in leadership from the University of St. Thomas, St. Paul, Minnesota.

Pierre Michiels, EDAC

Pierre Michiels is regional healthcare manager for Nurture by Steelcase, a graduate of the Haskayne School of Business in

Calgary in Alberta, Canada, and has had a 20-year career in sales and marketing. Mr. Michiels has worked with numerous organizations across Canada, helping them use their physical space to align with their business objectives. He has particular experience within the unique context of healthcare, linking patient and staff needs to current interior space strategies. Nurture by Steelcase is dedicated to making the healthcare experience better for the patient, the caregiver, and the care partner, by creating holistic healing environments.

Eleanor Lee, MAIBC, LEED AP, EDAC

Eleanor Lee is the director of project control and implementation with the Provincial Health Services Authority responsible for the design and technical specifications for the Children's and Women's Health Centre Redevelopment in British Columbia, Canada. Eleanor graduated from McGill University with a bachelor of commerce degree, after which she pursued graduate training in architecture at the University of British Columbia. A registered architect and LEED AP, Ms. Lee has been designing, planning, and constructing healthcare projects across the province for over 12 years.

Addie Johnson, EDAC

Addie Johnson is an environmental and organizational gerontologist, facilitating practices and design innovation in skilled nursing settings. She is a PhD candidate and fellow at UWM's Institute on Aging & Environment with a specialization in environment-aging relationships. Addie is the president of CARE WI (Changing Attitudes Regarding Elders), a Wisconsin-based network of individuals and organizations dedicated to person-centered care, and secretary for the SAGE Federation (Society for the Advancement of Gerontological Environments). She also serves on The Center for Health Design's EDAC (Evidence-Based Design Accreditation and Certification) Advisory Council. Addie has a bachelor of architecture degree from Kansas State University, a

minor in organizational development, and three graduate certifi-
cates: applied gerontology, mediation and negotiation, and nonprofit management. She is a co-developer of SAGE P.L.A.C.E.
(Programming for Living and Achieving Culture Change Environments), a pre-architectural programming workshop for long-
term care providers. Her professional experience includes: consulting with the Milwaukee Jewish Home & Care Center, web
database development for dementia design strategies, activity
therapist in Ottawa Co. Transitional Crossroad's traumatic brain
injury unit, and gerontological designer at Peacock Architects.
Addie has published and presents regularly on topics associated
with strategies for aging care provision.

Anjali Joseph, PhD, EDAC

Dr. Joseph is the director of research at The Center for Health
Design where she leads and coordinates research activities. Dr.
Joseph's areas of expertise include activity-friendly environments,
qualitative and quantitative research methods, and research applications in design.

Trained as an architect, Dr. Joseph is also a researcher and obtained
her PhD in architecture from the Georgia Institute of Technology
in Atlanta, Georgia. As part of her doctoral studies, she completed
her minor in heath systems from the School of Industrial Engineering at Georgia Tech. Dr. Joseph holds a bachelor degree in
architecture from the School of Planning and Architecture, New
Delhi, India. She completed her master's degree in architecture
from Kansas State University in Manhattan, Kansas.

Upali Nanda, PhD, EDAC

Upali Nanda is the vice president and director of research, therapeutic environments, at American Art Resources and is responsible
for investigating the role of art in creating healing environments.
Her research focuses on the effect of the designed environment

on human perception. Dr. Nanda received her PhD in architecture from Texas A&M University, with a certificate in health systems and design. She also holds a master of arts in architecture from National University of Singapore, with a bachelor degree from the School of Planning and Architecture, Delhi, India.